I0750115

The Third Book of the
GREAT MUSICIANS

Books by
Percy A. Scholes

The Listener's Guide to Music
The First Book of the Great Musicians
The Second Book of the Great Musicians
The Third Book of the Great Musicians
The Complete Book of the Great Musicians

The Third Book of the GREAT MUSICIANS

A Further Course in Appreciation for Young Readers

by

Percy A. Scholes

YESTERDAY'S CLASSICS

ITHACA, NEW YORK

This edition, first published in 2021 by Yesterday's Classics, an imprint of Yesterday's Classics, LLC, is an unabridged republication of the text originally published by Oxford University Press in 1923. For the complete listing of the books that are published by Yesterday's Classics, please visit www.yesterdaysclassics.com. Yesterday's Classics is the publishing arm of Gateway to the Classics which presents the complete text of hundreds of classic books for children at www.gatewaytotheclassics.com.

ISBN: 978-1-63334-130-2

Yesterday's Classics, LLC
PO Box 339
Ithaca, NY 14851

TO MUSIC TEACHERS

THIS *Third Book of the Great Musicians* in intention and plan so much resembles its two predecessors that no Preface is needed. But the author would like to take the opportunity of reminding teachers that his three books are meant to be placed *in the hands of the young people themselves,* not to be read to them, or to be read by the teacher and the contents re-told. The whole design of the books, with the abundant illustrations, and attractive 'lay-out' of the type, surely indicates the method of use.

In Class the books should be used much as school 'reading-books', each chapter being read and then (probably at some subsequent lesson) made the subject of discussion and illustrated by musical performance (the Gramophone will often be useful in this).

But besides the Class the author has had in view the individual young student of Piano or Violin, whose lesson does not allow time for 'appreciative' study, and who, without some such opportunity as these books attempt to give him, is often in danger of looking upon music rather narrowly—as a matter of mere 'lessons' and 'practice'. Music is just one of many means of human expression (and one of the best) and an implication of the simple humanity of music is one of the aims of the three *Books of the Great Musicians.*

I have once more to offer my thanks to Mr. Emery Walker. And to Mr. F. Page for assistance in finding illustrations, and to Mr. W. R. Anderson, editor of the monthly journal, *The Music Teacher,* for reading the proofs for me.

The Author

CONTENTS

BRAHMS

CHAPTER I

BRAHMS

1833-1897

On Having Musical Parents

Do you want to be a composer? If so, I hope your parents are fond of music. Look back over the list of musicians you have read about in the first two volumes of this work, and try to recall which of them inherited their musical talent. Here is the list:

Purcell.	Chopin.
Bach.	Field.
Handel.	Wagner.
Haydn.	Verdi.
Mozart.	Grieg.
Beethoven.	Sullivan.
Schubert.	Elgar.
Mendelssohn.	Macdowell.
Schumann.	Debussy.

If you think it over I believe that you will find that of all these composers there are only five of whom it is not related that one or both of the parents were musical. These five are Handel, Schumann, Wagner, Verdi, and Debussy. The fact that there have been some composers with unmusical parents is of course an encouragement to any of us whose parents are unmusical. If that boy Handel, whose father positively tried to stop his study of music, could yet develop into one of the world's greatest musicians, there is hope for everybody who seems to have been born with a musical brain and is willing to work. But, of course, the young musician who has inherited his gift, and has, moreover, parents who understand what he is striving after, has the better chance.

The Childhood of Brahms

Brahms had that better chance. His father was a musician. But the father himself had had no such chance, since *his* father was not a musician, and had even tried his best to prevent his having anything to do with music. The boy, however, took lessons by stealth, learned to play all the bowed instruments as well as the flute and the horn, and when he was old enough to earn his living became a professional double-bass player—one of the best in Hamburg.

Now a man who has had to struggle in youth generally does his best to make things easier for his children, and Brahms's father, finding his son inherited his talent for music, took care to give him good teachers in piano and composition. The mother, too, was musical, and used to play piano duets with her son.

The young Brahms very soon began to compose, and while still a boy occasionally made a little money by arranging marches and dances to be played by the little bands of the cafés. His father, in summer, used to form a party of six musicians who played in the open air for money, and for this party the boy sometimes composed music. The family, as you have observed already from what I have told you, was only a poor one, and all its members had to work hard. Brahms said that his best songs came into his head when he was brushing boots before dawn.

We nearly lost one of our greatest musicians before the world had heard anything of him, for once in the street a serious accident occurred: the lad fell and a cart went right over his chest. However, he recovered, and grew up a particularly sturdy man. At fifteen he gave a public concert, and this was the beginning of his being recognized as a musician of promise.

The Gipsy Fiddler

A great turning-point in Brahms's life came when he was a youth of twenty. He met the violinist Remenyi, who was a Hungarian, probably with gipsy blood, and who later became famous all over the world by playing his native melodies with great fire. Brahms accompanied this player at some concerts, and then they went on a concert tour together. Once when Beethoven's

'Kreutzer' Sonata was to be played they found the piano was tuned very low, so Brahms transposed its part a semitone higher, which rather impressed Remenyi. The Hungarian dances that Remenyi played attracted Brahms very strongly, and later he himself arranged a good many of these in a most effective way as piano duets; these are very delightful music, and all pianists who love bright, jolly, rhythmic tunes should play them.

Brahms Meets Joachim, Liszt, and Schumann

Up to this time the young Brahms was quite unknown to the leading musicians of the day. But at the concert at which he so cleverly transposed the sonata there was present the great violinist, Joachim, and when the concert was over he came and congratulated the players and offered to give them letters of introduction to Liszt at Weimar and Schumann at Düsseldorf.

They visited both these great musicians and were well received. Schumann especially was delighted with Brahms. He wrote to a publisher, saying that he really must bring out Brahms's compositions, and in a musical paper he wrote an article called *New Roads,* in which he hailed Brahms as a genius of great originality. The Schumanns used to have weekly musical parties, and Brahms played at these, and was accepted by every one as a 'coming' musician of great promise. He played some of Schumann's music in very masterly fashion. When you come to know a good deal of the music of both Schumann and Brahms you will find that it has much in common. There is no doubt that, like Remenyi,

Schumann was one of the great influences in Brahms's life. You already know that Schumann's brain gave way and that he died comparatively young, and his wife, you remember, was a fine pianist who toured Europe making her husband's genius known by her playing. All through Frau Schumann's long widowhood Brahms was her staunch friend. He looked on her almost as a mother, and she on him as a son, and she played his music wherever she went and helped to make it known.

Brahms as Choral Conductor

At twenty-one Brahms had already won such recognition that he had more than one good position opened to him. He accepted that of Director of the Court Concerts and the Choral Society of the Prince of Lippe-Ditmold. This gave him good experience, especially in choral training, and no doubt led to his composing such a great deal of fine choral music as he did now and in after-life. Of his choral works many are frequently heard in English-speaking countries, where they have become very popular.

The First Piano Concerto

When Brahms was twenty-six he brought out his first Pianoforte Concerto. It was performed at one of the Leipzig Gewandhaus Concerts, a very famous series, at which many great works have had their first hearing. There it had no success, but later Clara Schumann played it all over Germany and it became quite popular.

Twenty years later it was played again at the Leipzig concerts and had a triumphant success, but even to this day there are musicians in all parts of the world who do not greatly care for it. Some day you may yourself have a chance of hearing it and of forming your own opinion about it.

Brahms as Pianist and Piano Composer

Brahms himself played this work on its first appearance, and perhaps this was a little against it, for his playing, though in many ways very capable indeed, did not show that he sufficiently considered the nature of the instrument. He was very accurate and very vigorous, and got a big, full tone, but, as Schumann once put it, 'Brahms seemed to turn the piano into a full orchestra.' Many of his piano compositions show this same tendency. They would sound equally well, or almost so, rearranged for other instruments. You will gather better what I mean by this if you think of Chopin's music, which, of all piano music, is perhaps most thoroughly based upon a knowledge of what is effective *on a piano.*

Brahms and the Orchestra

Similarly, when writing for orchestra, Brahms did not get quite the full effect out of his orchestral instruments. If you hear one of his pieces, and then one of (say) Wagner or Elgar, you will feel that these latter composers get, so to speak, many more 'tone-colours' from their orchestral palette than does Brahms from his. Brahms's orchestral works, which include four Symphonies, are very fine indeed, but their scoring (that is, their laying out for the various instruments) is generally rather thick and not so clear and bright as that of most other great Composers. In this he takes somewhat after Schumann. Of both these Composers it has been said, 'He was more a draughtsman than a colourist.'

Brahms at Vienna

When Brahms was about forty he settled in Vienna, which, as you have already learned, has long been a great musical centre. He became conductor of the great choral society there, and got up fine performances of works of Bach, Beethoven, Schumann, and others.

One pleasure in Vienna was listening to the gipsy bands which played in the various public gardens. He used to stop and listen and clap loudly, and once was very delighted when the conductor, seeing him there, suddenly stopped the music, whispered to his men, and then struck up one of Brahms's own compositions. Earlier in this chapter you read something of the composer's love of the gipsy music.

A Lover of Light Music

Brahms was by no means opposed to light, pleasant music if it was good. He used to like to hear the famous dance music of Johann Strauss (Yo-han Strowss—pronounce the 'ow' as in 'cow'), who composed popular waltzes that were played all over Europe and America. When, at a musical party, Strauss's wife was persuading the musicians present to give her their autographs, Brahms wrote for her a few bars of the famous *Blue Danube Waltz* of Strauss and put under it the words, '*Not,* I am sorry to say, by your devoted friend, Johannes Brahms.'

Once, when a friend wrote to him complaining of the rather crude music played by the working men's brass bands and sung by the working men's choirs, he replied saying that he thought these things, though not so good as they might be, were nevertheless the only music then existing in which the working man was able to take part, and hence were to be encouraged.

Brahms's Advice to your Parents

He added something which some of my readers may care to read to their parents. He felt that it was a mistake that all the better-class children should learn the same one instrument, the Piano, and said, 'It is much to be wished that parents should have their children taught other instruments, such as Violin, 'Cello, Horn, Flute, or Clarinet, which would be the means of arousing interest in all kinds of music.'

Brahms's Requiem

One of Brahms's most important works that has not yet been mentioned is his 'German Requiem'. He wrote this after his mother's death, and much of it is very beautiful and touching. Generally speaking, 'Requiem' means a 'Requiem Mass' (i.e. the Roman Catholic service for the dead), but this 'Requiem' is, instead, a setting of texts from the Bible. The 'German Requiem' is constantly sung by choral societies in Britain and in America, and can sooner or later be heard by any of my readers who live in any large town.

Brahms's Death

There are no adventures in Brahms's life, and little to tell about it. In 1897 his dear friend, Schumann's widow, died, and at her funeral he caught cold, fell ill himself, and died at the age of sixty-four. He was buried in Vienna, in the same cemetery as Beethoven and Schubert.

What Brahms Was Like

Brahms was a big, strong, stout man, who dressed carelessly, and loved the open air. He was very athletic, and loved of all things to go on long walking tours or mountain expeditions. At the seaside he used to swim a great deal and liked to dive for coins thrown into the water by his friends. When he was a boy he had a lovely voice, but he spoilt it by using it too much when it was breaking, and so his voice as a man was gruff.

He loved children and was always playing with them. Once in a Swiss city he was seen going through all the streets, with the five-year-old daughter of a friend on his back, and from Italy an American lady wrote to her friends, 'We saw Brahms on the hotel verandah at Domodossola, and what do you think! He was down on all fours, with three children on his back, riding him as a horse.' In the street he constantly stopped to talk to the children, and they would follow him about.

Brahms paid very little attention to other people's praise or blame, and just went on his own way, behaving as he liked and composing as he liked and what he liked. He was often rude to people, and hurt their feelings, especially if they came to him with praise on their lips. Once when he was lying under a tree in a garden a stranger came up and began to flatter him, so Brahms said, 'I think, sir, you must be mistaken. No doubt you are looking for my brother, the composer. Most unfortunately he has just gone out for a walk, but if you will make haste and run along that path through the wood and up the hill, perhaps you will be able to catch him.'

Brahms was always very fond of a joke and did not like very 'starchy' people. Nobody could ever persuade him to come to England, because, as he said, he would have to be always respectably dressed. There is an anecdote about Brahms which illustrates both his kindness of heart and his humour. When he had become a fairly well-to-do man and went to visit his parents at Hamburg, he called the attention of his father, before he left, to his own old copy of Handel's *Saul.* 'Dear father,' he said, 'if things go badly with one the best consolation is always in music. Read carefully in my old *Saul,* and you'll find what you need.' And when the old fellow did look into *Saul* what did he find there?—Bank-notes between the pages!

Brahms and Wagner

Many people who objected to Wagner's music tried to pit that of Brahms against it. They maintained that Wagner's music was very unpleasant, whereas that of Brahms was 'pure' and wholesome. But Brahms himself took no part in this and expressed the greatest admiration for the music of Wagner, although Wagner himself did not care for his. Of course, there is the greatest difference between Wagner's music and that of Brahms. For one thing, Wagner wrote for the stage, while Brahms, on the other hand, never wrote an opera or music drama in his life, as he did not feel drawn to this sort of composition.

Despite the difference in their music both Brahms and Wagner are much indebted to the same inspiration—Beethoven. You have already learned how Beethoven's works excited and inspired Wagner, and now you may learn that they also inspired Brahms. In the first volume of this book you have learned to understand the differences between 'classical' and 'romantic' music. We may say that Beethoven is both classical and romantic, and that Brahms continued his work more on the classical side, and Wagner on the romantic side. Beethoven, as you know, wrote nine Symphonies, and when Brahms wrote his first somebody called it 'Beethoven's Tenth'. Brahms loved Beethoven's works, and could play from memory almost any one of them you cared to ask for.

Like Beethoven, Brahms wrote a good deal of fine chamber music. He also wrote a large number of beautiful songs (more than 200), and a good deal of piano music. In many of his pieces you find several conflicting rhythms going on at the same time. You might look out for this when you hear some of his instrumental music.

Brahms loved Folk Songs and Folk Dances, and a good deal of his music is influenced by these.

QUESTIONS

(To See Whether You Remember the Chapter and Understand It)

1. Without looking back at the beginning of the chapter, write down on a sheet of paper the names of all the musicians you can remember who have been discussed in the two previous volumes of this book. Leave a little space under each name, and then write

under each what you remember as to the parents being musical or otherwise.

2. What do you remember about Beethoven's father and grandfather?

3. Was Brahms born rich?

4. Tell all you remember about that Hungarian violinist whom Brahms met when he was a youth.

5. Do you remember any other great violinist he met?

6. What do you know about Brahms's relations with Schumann?

7. Say what you know (a) about Brahms's Piano Playing style, and Piano Composing style, and (b) about his Orchestration.

8. Where did Brahms settle in middle life?

9. When Brahms heard a good Waltz played by a band in the street did he turn up his nose and say 'What rubbish!' do you suppose? Or do you think he gave the band sixpence? What is *your* idea about 'light music'? Do you like (a) *bad* light music, or (b) *all* light music, or (c) only *good* light music? Have you any idea what makes the difference between good and bad light music? Can you mention any English composer of good light music?

10. What was Brahms's advice to parents?

11. Tell what you know about 'Requiems' in general, and Brahms's Requiem in particular.

12. How old (roughly) was Brahms when he died?

13. Was Brahms a well-dressed man? How did he spend his holidays? Some people did not like him; was he the sort of fellow *you* would have liked? Why? or Why not? (as the case may be).

14. In what way did Brahms continue the work of Beethoven?

THINGS TO DO

(For School and Home)

1. If you have a Gramophone try to get some records of works of Brahms.

2. If you have a Pianola try to get some rolls of his music.

3. If you have neither (or even if you have) try to find some friend who can play you some of Brahms's music, or sing you some of his songs.

4. Look out for the announcement of the performance of any of Brahms's works in your town, and go to hear them. If they are Choral or Orchestral works perhaps you can get in to the rehearsal, so that at the concert you will be hearing the music for a second time, and so understanding it better.

CHAPTER II

CÉSAR FRANCK

1822-1890

IF you had seen César Franck in the streets of Paris probably you would have thought little of him—a short man with grey side-whiskers, and a face making queer grimaces, an overcoat too big and trousers too small. But if you had followed him to the church to which he was hurrying, crept up the dark stairs behind him to the organ gallery, and seen him seated at his fine instrument and surrounded by some of his admiring friends and pupils, you would have had a different idea of him. People who have seen him at those moments, as he prepared the stops of his organ and broke into some wonderful improvization, say that 'he seemed to be surrounded by music as by a halo.' The great musician Liszt once visited him there and came away lost in astonishment and saying that to have heard old Bach himself must have been a similar experience.

Franck's Sincerity

It was not only Franck's skill that so much impressed people who heard him; it was his sincerity, too. We say

CÉSAR FRANCK

of a man sometimes, 'he means every word he says,' and people might have said of Franck 'he means every note he plays.' There was in Franck's playing and his composing nothing put in just for effect or to win applause; he did not compose to make money, but to express his true thoughts and feelings, and these were often very deep.

Perhaps you have not yet heard any of Franck's music, but you will some day have the chance, for it is now much performed. If you hear the fine *Symphony* or the *Violin and Piano Sonata,* or the *String Quartet,* or the *Prelude, Choral, and Fugue* for Piano, or the *Prelude, Aria, and Finale* for the same instrument, or any of the *Organ Pieces,* or the great Choral work *The Beatitudes,* I think you will feel the truth of what I have just said. But you must be prepared to study them a little, or to hear them two or three times before making up your mind about them, for great works like this are not to be thoroughly understood the very first time we hear them. If you can get some pianist to play you one of the piano works do so, but, before he begins, get him to go through the work with you, playing you the few chief tunes and showing you how the whole thing is made out of these.

Franck's Early Life

Franck was born at Liège, in Belgium, on December 10, 1822, which was the very day on which Beethoven wrote the last note of what is, perhaps, his greatest work, his Mass in D. This is worth remembering, because, more even than Brahms, Franck was the continuer of Beethoven, carrying further Beethoven's style and his ideas in the Sonata and Symphony just mentioned, and in other works.

Franck's father was a business man, and, seeing his son had musical talent, wished him to turn it to account. When the boy was ten he took him for a tour in Belgium, giving concerts everywhere, and when he was fourteen he took him to Paris to be trained at the great Conservatoire there.

Young Franck at the Conservatoire

When Franck had been a year at the Conservatoire he entered for a competition in piano-playing. He played very brilliantly the set piece he had prepared, and was then given a piece to play at sight. Some queer idea that came into his head prompted him to do a clever yet foolish thing. Instead of just playing the piece as it stood he transposed it three notes lower—and played it perfectly with this added difficulty. The judges said he had broken the rules by doing this, and so they could not give him the prize, but old Cherubini (Ker-oo-*bee*-ny), the head of the Conservatoire, said such a feat ought, after all, not to go unrewarded, so they invented a special distinction for Franck, and conferred on him the 'Grand Prix d'Honneur', a prize which had never been given before and has never been given since.

A year or two later, at an Organ competition at the Conservatoire, Franck did another strange thing.

Amongst other tests, the students had to improvise a Sonata on a 'subject' given them by the examiners, and then a Fugue on another subject, also given. When Franck came to improvise the Fugue, it struck him that the Sonata subject and the Fugue subject would work together, so he brought them both in, and made a long and elaborate composition out of them that surprised the examiners, but compelled them to say again that the regulations were broken. However, they gave him the Second Prize.

Franck Leaves the Conservatoire

About this time Franck's father removed him from the Conservatoire. He wanted him to be a piano 'virtuoso' (that is, a great performer, travelling everywhere and giving recitals) and also to compose piano music that would have a large sale and bring in much money. This, however, did not attract Franck, who did not care for fame, or desire more money than was really necessary to live upon comfortably, and before long this difference of opinion, and one upon another question, drew father and son rather apart.

He Gets Married

The other question was that of Franck's marriage. When he was 26 he fell in love with a young actress and wished to marry her. His father objected, but Franck was not going to give way, and was supported in his intention by a good priest who was fond of him.

This was in 1848, when Paris was in revolution. To get to the church the young couple had to climb over the barricades that the revolutionaries had set up in the streets, but the armed men who were guarding them helped them over and let them pass.

Pupils were scarce just then, for the city was, of course, in a very disturbed state; thus Franck began his married life in some poverty. However, shortly afterwards, the priest who had helped him at the time of his marriage was appointed to a church where there was a fine organ, and he made Franck the organist. This delighted Franck, who was a great lover of the organ, and, as a very devout Christian, was never happier than when taking his part in the church service. Later Franck was appointed to a larger church with a still finer organ, the new basilica of Sainte-Clothilde.

A Disappointment

Every composer has some disappointments, and Franck had more than most. About this time he spent all the time he could spare, for over a year, in writing an Opera called *The Farmer's Man.* Often he sat up almost all night, working at it, and when it was done he was quite worn out and his brain was so tired that he could hardly think. Yet he never got it performed. But note this—years after, when somebody mentioned it, he said he had come to see that it was not worth very much after all, and he should certainly never have allowed it to be printed.

This is what often happens: one works at a thing, expecting to make a great success and then, instead, comes failure. For a time one is cast down, and not till long after does one realize that the failure was a blessing in disguise. But perhaps no good work is ever really wasted, and one realizes in time that though the thing itself failed, one is the better for the effort and for what it taught one. So although Franck never saw the Opera performed, in writing it he had gained strength as a composer, and no doubt afterwards profited by this.

Later Franck had a little greater success as an Opera composer, but Instrumental Music and Choral Music, not Theatre Music, were really the lines in which he was fitted to excel.

A Modest Life

Many other disappointments came to Franck in the course of his life, but where other men would have been cast down he just went quietly on. Largely his time was occupied in going about Paris and giving Piano lessons here and there, or Singing lessons at schools, or Organ lessons at the Conservatoire, or, on Sundays and Saints' Days, in playing at his church. He rose at half-past five and 'worked *for himself*' (as he put it) for two hours. Then he had breakfast and hurried off to do his teaching. By 'working for himself' he meant composing or studying, for, busy as he was, he never dropped composition and study.

Franck as the Friend of Young Composers

In the evening when he got home he would have dinner and then, often, there would gather round him a group of young musicians who wanted his help and advice. There were at that time in Paris some of these young men who felt that the teaching of Composition at the Conservatoire did not give them what they wanted, since it was so largely concerned with writing in the Operatic style, and they were more interested in Instrumental music, in which France had dropped a good deal behind.

These men realized that in Franck they had a man who could guide them and they liked to get his advice, and to bring their compositions to him, for him to suggest to them where these could be improved and strengthened. But Franck was very modest, and would sometimes play *his* music to *them,* and ask what they thought of it, and if they made suggestions that seemed to be sound, he would accept them and put them into practice. Thus there grew up a sort of Franck 'school', as we say—using the word 'school' to mean a set of people more or less influenced by the same ideas and having much the same way of looking at things.

The 'Schola Cantorum'

After Franck's death there sprang out of his teaching a school in the other sense of the word—an institution where music was taught much on the lines of his teaching.

This still exists and is called the 'Schola Cantorum'. Its head is a composer called Vincent d'Indy (*Van*-son *Dan*-dy is as near as I can get the pronunciation, in English spelling). D'Indy has written a fine book about his old master, Franck, and a good deal of what I am telling you now is, of course, what I have learnt from that book.

One thing which they do at this school is to go back to the works of Palestrina and Bach, and others of the greatest writers of the best periods of old-time music, and to learn from them as much as they can. Similarly they study the old Plainsong (the traditional chants of the church). In this way they feel they are laying a solid foundation, and after such training as this their pupils may write in as modern a way as they like but will not be out of touch with the past. For of course the present-day music must be founded on that of past days, and future music, we may be sure, will be to some extent founded on that of the present.

Some of Franck's Sayings

When Franck was talking to some of his pupils he would say, 'Don't try to do a great deal; rather try to do a little *well*.' And when he set them an exercise in composition he expected them to work it in all possible ways, and show him the best working they could make—'Bring me the results of *many* trials, which you can honestly say represent the *very best* you can do.'

Then he would add, 'Don't think you can learn

anything from my corrections of faults of which you were aware—unless before bringing the exercises you had done your level best to correct them yourself.'

All these are sound maxims, and should be applied by all students. It really comes to this—'Don't rely on your teachers to do things for you that you can do yourself. Learn for yourself everything you possibly can do, and then let your teacher's help be *additional to that.*' This applies to Piano practice as much as to Composing, and, indeed, to every possible subject of study.

A Concert That Failed

When Franck was 65 his pupils and friends felt it to be a wrong thing that some of his best works had yet hardly been heard in public. So they got up a subscription to pay for a great concert of his works. A famous Parisian conductor was to direct the first part and Franck the second. But the famous conductor got quite muddled in the middle of one of the pieces, and conducted it at double its proper speed, so that it broke down. And as for Franck, when his turn came, he was so busy thinking of the music he had written that he did not pay enough attention to helping the singers and players, so that he, too, made rather a mess of things. (It often happens that fine composers are poor conductors.)

When the concert was over Franck's pupils gathered round him and said how sorry they felt that things had gone so badly, but he replied, 'No, no, my dear boys; you are really too exacting; for my part I was *quite* satisfied.'

I suppose he heard the music in his mind as he meant it to be, and not as it was really performed. And it was a great treat to the dear old man to hear any sort of performance of his works, since they had up to then been so much neglected.

Franck's Death

When Franck was 68 his beautiful String Quartet was performed, and the audience applauded very heartily. Franck could not believe his ears when he heard the applause, and thought it was all for the performers. But it was applause for him. And he had to go on to the platform and bow, and to be made much of. When he got home he said, 'There, you see, the public is beginning to understand me at last!'

It is pleasant to think that this had at last happened, but success came only just in time, for later in the same year he was knocked down by an omnibus. He seemed to recover, and went about his work as usual, but in a few months he was taken ill and died.

He had written three beautiful Chorales for the organ, and wanted very much to be able to go to the church to try them over, but this was not possible, and they were lying on the bed when the priest came to give him the last comforts of religion.

His was a noble, hard-working, self-sacrificing life.

What Franck's Music Is Like

It is always difficult to describe music in words. Franck's we may say was very fervent, and very pure, and often very tender, and generally mystical. By mystical, what do we mean? It is as difficult to describe mysticism as I just said it was to describe music, but I think I can make you understand if I say that in a piece of Franck's you can generally feel that its composer was not just thinking of the things around him, but in a sort of vision was peering forward into a life beyond what our eyes can see.

QUESTIONS

(To See Whether You Remember the Chapter and Understand It)

1. When and where was Franck born?

2. What great musicians were then alive? Think of four or five, and say whether they were old men nearing the end of their work, or young ones beginning their lives.

3. Where was Franck trained in music?

4. Repeat any anecdotes you can remember of his work as an examination candidate.

5. What traits in Franck's nature came out in his disagreement with his father?

6. What sort of a life did Franck lead in Paris?

7. What did he mean by working *for himself?*

8. How did he influence younger musicians?

9. What is the Schola Cantorum, and who is the head of it?

10. Repeat some of Franck's advice to young composers.

11. Was Franck an old man or a young one when he died?

12. Try to give in words some idea of Franck's music.

THINGS TO DO

1. Of course the chief thing to do is to hear and study some of Franck's music. Try to find a good pianist who can play some of it, and get him (or her) to play you the 'subjects' of a piece before playing the piece as a whole, and to show you how the piece is made out of its subjects.

2. Get a Gramophone record of something of Franck's, e.g. his *Chasseur maudit* (or *Accursed Hunter*). This is published by the Columbia Company, and they give away with it a leaflet telling the story Franck has illustrated in his music.

3. Be on the watch for the announcement of any performance of the great Symphony by Franck. If you see it announced try to get somebody to explain it to you and to play you the 'subjects', before you hear the

performance. Do the same with the Violin and Piano Sonata. Both these are very beautiful works that you are sure to like as soon as you really know them.

4. Older readers might get d'Indy's book on Franck (translated by Mrs. Newmarch and published by John Lane), and read it carefully.

CHAPTER III

RUSSIAN MUSIC

RUSSIA is a big place—twice as big as the whole of Europe, one sixth of the world's land surface! And, of course, so big a country, lying partly in Europe, and partly in Asia, extending from the Arctic Ocean almost to India, and from Central Europe to China, has amongst its inhabitants people of many different nationalities. So when I write a chapter about Russian Music I must narrow down my subject, or it would become not a chapter, but a book. Roughly speaking, then, this chapter will leave out Asiatic Russia altogether, and will discuss, quite simply, the music of European Russia, and even about that will only give a few main facts, such as everybody who cares about music should know.

Russian Folk Music

As you have learnt in *The First Book of the Great Musicians,* all peoples have their Folk Music, and of course the Russians have theirs. Naturally in so vast a country the Folk Music is of many different kinds. If you have heard a few English, Scottish, Irish, and Welsh Folk Songs you can generally, ever after, tell whether any British Folk Song or Folk Dance Tune you may hear comes from England, Scotland, Ireland, or Wales, which shows us at once how people in different countries, or different parts of a country, produce differing styles of Folk Music. And if we have several different styles in these tiny British Isles, of course the Russians, in their vast country, must have still more. Not much has been known of the Russian Folk Music by people in the east of Europe until lately, but Beethoven got hold of some Russian Folk Tunes long ago, and used them in his famous Rasoumovsky String Quartets, so they have not been altogether overlooked.

What the Music Is Like

Since there are so many different styles of Russian Folk Tunes, it is difficult to describe them in a general way, but perhaps we can say with truth that, to us, they generally seem to be either very mournful or very excited and gay. Here is one of the qualities of the Russian character. Russians, as their literature shows, are a very up-and-down people—easily depressed into sadness and just as easily excited into joy.

At various periods the Russian priests have taught that music is a sin, and have tried to banish it, but nobody in any country can get rid of music, because music is a part of human nature, and so Russian Folk Ballads and Folk Dances have gone on, carrying down with them, from generation to generation, the legends of olden days and stories from early Russian history.

Russian Church Music

The orthodox Russian religion is that branch of Christianity which we call the Greek Church. This looks upon Constantinople as its headquarters, as the Roman Catholic Church looks upon Rome, and uses the Greek language in its services as the Roman Catholic Church uses Latin. Like the Roman Catholic Church, the Greek Church has both old Plain Chant melodies that have come down from the early days of Christianity, and also music made for it by skilful composers.

The singing in some of the Russian churches has long had a reputation for great beauty. It is not accompanied by instruments, and one very remarkable thing is that the Russian basses can sing very low notes—far and away lower than any notes our basses can sing.

So far the music we have been talking about is what we may call the real Russian music—the Songs and Dance Tunes that have grown up in the Russian villages, the Church Plain Chant that has grown up in the Eastern Church and come down from the early days of Christianity in Russia, and the composed Church Music. Much of this latter, however, though it is by Russian composers, and written for the Russian churches, has yet been influenced by the style of Church Music in other parts of Europe.

Italian Music in Russia

We now come, however, to music that was not merely influenced by the music of other parts of Europe, but brought complete from them, music that, though performed in Russia, was not in any sense Russian. During the eighteenth century the Imperial Family, who loved splendour of every kind, used to send to Italy for some of the best Italian performers, and used to have performances of Italian Operas at court. As you have already learnt, Italy is the native country of Opera, so it was natural to send there for the musicians to compose and perform it. In this way Italian Opera became popular amongst the aristocracy, both in Petrograd and Moscow.

The First Real Russian Composer

But cultivated Russian musical people began to wish for a real Russian composer, and by and by he came. His name was GLINKA. He was born in 1804. His father was a rich man, and at his country house used to receive many visitors. When he had a big party of these in the house he would send a message to Glinka's uncle, who lived a few miles away, and who kept a private Orchestra for his entertainment. Then the uncle's Orchestra would come over, and little Glinka was in a heaven of joy, and if he was not watched would pick up an instrument and try to join in the music.

GLINKA

His governess taught him the piano and one of the orchestral players taught him the violin. When he went to school at Petrograd he had piano lessons from the famous Irish musician, of whom you have read in *The Second Book of the Great Musicians,* John Field. Then when he was a young man he was sent to Italy for some years, for the good of his health, and there he heard a lot of music, and took regular lessons in composition. At first his compositions imitated those of the Italians, but at last he realized that he was wrong in this, and that as a Russian he would never write really good music by imitating composers of such different national feeling from his own as the Italians. So, after visiting Germany and having some lessons in the technique of composition there, he returned to Russia, where he began to compose music with Russian feeling in it, rather than either Italian or German feeling.

'A Life for the Czar'

The first great work that he wrote was the opera, *A Life for the Czar*, which tells a story from Russian history, the story of a peasant who was forced to act as a guide to an army that was coming to attack that of the Czar, but who led it into the forest, so that the Czar might be saved, although he knew the enemy would kill him when they found that he had tricked them. A good deal of the music of this opera was much in the style of the Russian Folk-Music, rather than in the style of the Italian or German operas. So both in its subject and in its music *A Life for the Czar* may be truly called a national work.

This opera became very popular with patriotic Russians and when, in 1886, the fiftieth year after its composition came to be celebrated, every theatre in Russia made a point of performing it, and so doing honour to its composer—the first really national composer Russia ever had.

Glinka wrote another opera *(Russian and Ludmilla)* and some orchestral music, chamber music, and piano music. There is no need to describe this other music here. For the moment I just want to impress upon your mind the name of Glinka as the first really national composer, and therefore the founder of the Russian 'School' of composition. He died in 1857, so he did not have a very long life. You may sometimes hear his music at concerts, but not very often.

Dargomysky and 'The Five'

Another early Russian composer, born a little later than Glinka, was DARGOMYSKY, and then we come to a group of composers, who worked together in the effort to produce a real 'School' of Russian music. They were always spoken of as THE FIVE. I am going to give their names and dates. You need not learn the dates, but they will be there for you to refer to whenever you want them. The names, however, you ought to learn, so that when you hear any of their music you will be able to listen to it with a little more interest, knowing it to be the work of one of this little band of comrades who set out to bring into existence a body of real Russian music—

BALAKIREF (1836-1910). The leader of the 'School'.

CUI (1835-1918). Partly of French descent.

BORODIN (1834-1887), wrote the Opera, *Prince Igor*.

MOUSSORGSKY (1839-1881), wrote the opera *Boris Godounof*.

RIMSKY-KORSAKOF (1844-1908), the first Russian to write a Symphony.

From a glance at that list you will at any rate get into your mind the fact that the famous 'Five' were all born in the eighteen-thirties or eighteen-forties, and that one or two of them lived almost down to your own time. Sometimes instead of 'The Five', these composers are known by the very grand title of 'The Invincible Band'.

They really deserve such a title, for they wrote some very great works, and it was *their* works which, when they began to be performed in Britain in the last years of the nineteenth century and the first years of the twentieth, really proved to British people that Russia was to be looked upon as an important musical country.

QUESTIONS

(To See Whether You Remember the Chapter and Understand It)

1. Roughly, how big is Russia?

2. And what deduction about Folk Music can we draw from this?

3. Tell anything you remember about Russian Church Music.

4. How did Italy come to influence Russia in music?

5. And who first cast off the Italian influence?

6. Whom do we mean by THE FIVE?

7. Give their names, if you can.

THINGS TO DO

1. If you have a Gramophone, and are so magnificently rich that you can afford to buy any records that you want, search the Catalogue and you will find some pieces by Cui, Borodin, Rimsky-Korsakof, and

Moussorgsky (and, perhaps, by the time this is printed, other composers). Get these records and learn to know them thoroughly.

2. Look out for concerts where music by any of the composers mentioned is to be given, and attend them.

3. Ask your English teacher to go through this chapter with the form, and then to set an essay on 'Russian Music'.

TCHAIKOVSKY

CHAPTER IV

TCHAIKOVSKY

1840-1893

I AM giving a whole chapter to Tchaikovsky, not that he is the most important Russian composer, but because at the present time he is the Russian composer whose music you are most likely to hear often, and in whom, therefore, you are most likely to be interested.

Tchaikovsky's Boyhood and Youth

Tchaikovsky does not appear to have been a specially musical boy. He learnt the piano, as other boys do, and when he went to the university he sang in the choral society there. Then when his education was finished he sometimes improvised dance music, for his own pleasure and to please his friends, but did not take music very seriously.

At twenty-one, however, he suddenly 'woke up' to music. He was then a civil servant at Petrograd, but he began to take lessons in composing, and to work hard at musical study generally. After a time he decided to throw up his place in the civil service and go in thoroughly for music, studying at the Conservatory at Petrograd. At first he was poor, for he had now abandoned his means of earning a comfortable living, and as his father had misfortunes he could not afford to help his son very much. Music-teaching, however, brought him in a small income, and this made things a little easier. He did well at the Conservatory, and won a silver medal for a work he composed. When he was twenty-six, the Conservatory of Moscow gave him a post on its staff as a teacher of composition, and then he felt that, though still poor, he was really started in life.

The head of the Petrograd Conservatory was a very famous musician, Anton Rubinstein, the great pianist, of whom you may have heard, and the head of the Moscow Conservatory was his brother, Nicholas Rubinstein. Nicholas believed in Tchaikovsky, and did all he could to help him by bringing his works forward, and getting them performed.

The 'Musician's Temperament'

All his life Tchaikovsky was very 'nervy'. Many musicians are easily excited into joy, and easily depressed into gloom. This comes from their sensitive natures, without which they could not be musicians, and if they suffer from ill health (as Tchaikovsky did), and do not make a steady effort to obtain self-control (as Tchaikovsky probably did not), their nervous temperament gives them a good deal of trouble all through their life. Tchaikovsky was often saddened by not receiving the recognition he felt his work deserved, but when he was about thirty-seven something happened which cheered him and helped him all the rest of his life.

A Generous Friend

A rich woman who loved music had engaged a young violinist to play to her and to organize musical performances in her house. Some of the music they played was the music of Tchaikovsky, of which she was very fond. The violinist used to tell her sometimes about the rather sad life of Tchaikovsky, whose pupil he had been at the Conservatory of Moscow; how he had difficulty in making a living, and could not compose as much as he wished because he had to spend time in giving music-lessons. The lady, who had at one time herself been very poor, wrote to Tchaikovsky and persuaded him to let her help him, and at last offered to allow him a yearly income so that he might be free to compose, and so to give to the world the best that was in him.

After some demur Tchaikovsky accepted this offer, and for a time lived a good deal abroad, in Switzerland and Italy, gradually building up a better state of health, and spending his time in composition. Sometimes, when he returned to Russia, he would spend long periods at one or other of the country houses of this good woman, working quietly and happily.

A curious thing is that Tchaikovsky and his benefactress never met, or at any rate never but in the most passing way—just, perhaps, a 'Good evening' as they saw one another at some concert, and very rarely even that. They corresponded a great deal, however, and Tchaikovsky's letters to this lady are many of them now published and are very interesting as giving an account of his life and showing how he composed his various works, but it seems to have been a point with his benefactress, who was a widow living a very retired life, that her good works should be done at a distance. The name of the good widow, who did almost as much for music as if she had been herself a composer, was Nadejda von Meck.

Success at Last

After years of struggle great success at last came to Tchaikovsky. His compositions, which had at first aroused opposition, became accepted everywhere, and when Nicholas Rubinstein died the authorities of the Moscow Conservatory offered Tchaikovsky his post. But he refused this, for he felt that if he took it he would no longer have time and energy and freedom of mind for his composition.

At last he wrote an Opera which brought him great fame—*Eugen Oniegin.* His health began to improve and his nerves to become stronger as he felt that at last he had made a success of life. Mostly he lived quietly in the country, working hard at his compositions, but sometimes he took tours abroad, conducting his works at great concerts in various cities, and being welcomed everywhere. Several times he came to England and conducted his music at the concerts of the Philharmonic Society in London. He was invited to go to Cambridge to receive an honorary degree of Doctor of Music, and was made much of there. He also went to America and conducted in New York and other cities.

Tchaikovsky's Early Death

Tchaikovsky died far too early—in his fifty-third year. A professor of Russian in one of our English Universities has told me this story. When this professor was a youth he was a musician, and studied in the Conservatory of Budapest. One day a great concert was held at which Tchaikovsky appeared and conducted, and when the concert was over the students carried him shoulder high in triumph back on to the stage which he had left when the music was over.

As they did so, one of the students began to express the joy of the gathering by playing the Tubular Bells, and Tchaikovsky exclaimed with alarm to some of those near him that it was a bad omen, for in Russia when they carry a dead body to the grave the church bells are rung. This, of course, shows what a nervous, fanciful man he was, and the worst is that superstitious ideas of this sort have a way of coming true, because people brood upon them, and so in the end weaken their health.

A little time after, as Tchaikovsky was travelling by train in Russia, he pointed to a village churchyard as the train passed it, and told his friends who were with him, 'I shall be buried there, and as the trains go by people will point out the grave.'

A few days later he drank a glass of unfiltered water, fell ill with cholera, and quickly died. I do not know whether he was buried in that village churchyard. I hope he was, and that as the trains go by the passengers do sometimes point to it and say, 'Tchaikovsky is buried there,' and feel grateful for the music he wrote, which, though it is not amongst the very greatest, has brought pleasure to people in every part of the civilized world, and will do so for a long time to come.

What Tchaikovsky's Music Is Like

Now about Tchaikovsky's music. Some of this you have probably heard, such as, for instance, the *Nutcracker Suite* (often called by the French name of *Casse-noisette).* If you have heard only this piece (or, rather, string of pieces) you will understand what I mean when I say that Tchaikovsky's music is of a kind that anybody can understand at once.

This does not necessarily mean that it is good music or poor music. It means that it is *simple* music—with clear tunes for its 'subjects' or 'themes', with these clearly treated, with harmonies put to them such as do not puzzle one at all, and with orchestration of a kind that any one can enjoy at a first hearing. This Suite is particularly easy to take in as soon as one hears it, because it has no long 'movements', but is just a set of little pieces in which the mind cannot possibly lose its way.

The Symphonies

In Tchaikovsky's bigger pieces, such as his Symphonies, there are the same qualities, but, of course, these bigger pieces express deeper thoughts and are more elaborate in their structure than the little pieces of the *Nutcracker Suite.* In some of their 'movements' you will feel Tchaikovsky's joyousness and in others his depression. Sometimes you will be able to feel what a sensitive and even feverishly excitable temperament he had. The best way to describe Tchaikovsky's music is to say that it is very 'emotional'. The Symphonies most often heard are the Fourth, Fifth, and Sixth. The Sixth has a name—*The Pathetic Symphony*. It is very popular at orchestral concerts in Britain and America.

Other orchestral pieces of Tchaikovsky's are in the form of Tone Poems—pieces in which the composer tries to express in music the emotions connected with some series of incidents, much as a poet might do in words. Thus Tchaikovsky has one tone poem on the subject of *Romeo and Juliet.*

Then there are three Concertos for Piano, and one for Violin, a number of Operas, some dance music for the stage (such as the Ballet, *The Sleeping Princess*), some Chamber Music, and a great number of Piano pieces and Songs.

You can get a good deal of Tchaikovsky's music in the form of Gramophone records.

QUESTIONS

(To See Whether You Remember the Chapter and Understand It)

1. When was Tchaikovsky born?

2. And how long before your time did he die?

3. Was he a clever musical boy, like many of the composers of whom you have read?

4. Where did he study?

5. What sort of a temperament had he?

6. Tell how his early struggles ended.

7. Did Tchaikovsky die young or old?

8. Try if you can give any sort of a general description of Tchaikovsky's musical style.

9. And mention any music of his which you know.

THINGS TO DO

1. If you have a Gramophone, get some of Tchaikovsky's music as records.

2. If you play the Piano fairly well you might get the *Nutcracker Suite (Casse-noisette)* in a piano arrangement.

3. Make a point of hearing Tchaikovsky's music at concerts whenever you can. It is frequently performed.

4. When a week has elapsed from the day you read this chapter, jot down, roughly, on paper, a note of all you can remember of it. Then read the chapter again, and find out what you had forgotten.

CLAVICHORD

VIRGINAL

CHAPTER V

CLAVICHORD—HARPSICHORD—PIANOFORTE

One of the words at the head of this chapter you know quite well. The other two words you have surely heard. You ought, if you are a pianist, to know something about Clavichords and Harpsichords, because some of your music was written not for the piano but for one or other of these instruments. And besides, people are now reviving the Clavichord and Harpsichord, and you may any day have a chance of hearing one of them, when you will want to know something about it. Before we go any further you may like to see what these instruments look like. So please study the pictures of them.

Now let me explain the principle. Clavichord, Harpsichord, and Piano are alike in this—they all have wires and they all have keys.

And they are unlike in this—the way the keys bring the sound out of the wires.

Suppose we take a wire and stretch it tight over something, like this—

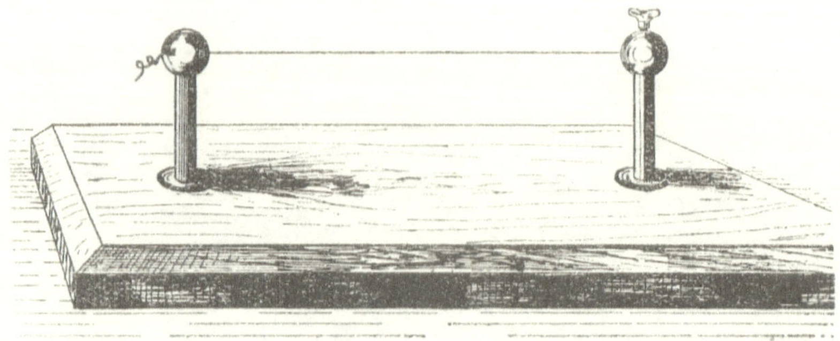

and then begin to consider how music can be got out of it. I suppose there are two main ways—

(a) we can *pluck* the wire with our fingers;

(b) we can *hammer* it with something.

A fairly common plucked-string instrument is the ZITHER.

A fairly common hammered-string instrument is the DULCIMER.

The Zither

Here is a picture of a Zither—

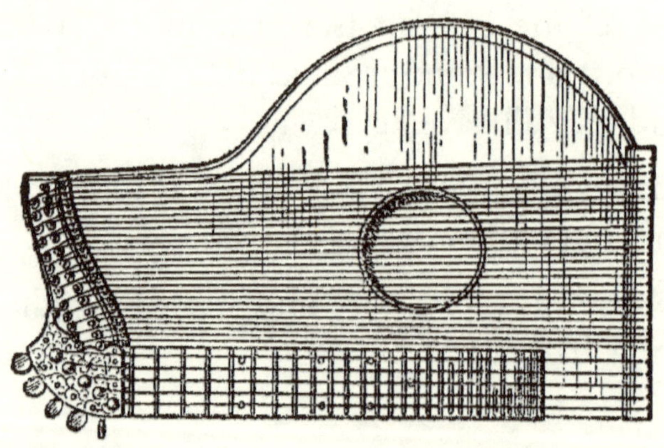

Here the player plucks the strings with his fingers, or with a little piece of metal called a Plectrum. There are a number of strings of different lengths, long strings for the low notes and short strings for the high notes.

The Dulcimer

Now let us look at a Dulcimer—

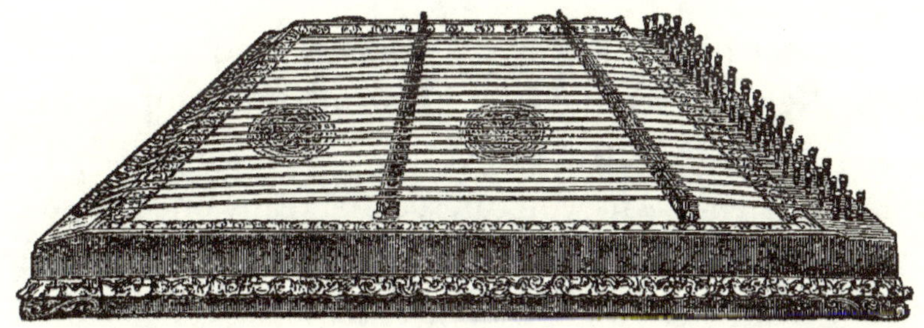

A Dulcimer player knocks the strings with two little hammers (one in each hand). Again, there are long strings for low notes and short strings for high ones.

Now, in a way (I am not speaking very accurately, but only trying to give you a good general idea)—

A **Harpsichord** = a mechanical Zither.

A **Pianoforte** = a mechanical Dulcimer.

What a Harpsichord is Like

The **Harpsichord** is a kind of Keyboard-Zither. Each note of the keyboard has at the farther end of it a little piece of wood called a Jack. And each Jack has in it a Quill. And when the note is pressed down by the player, up goes the Jack and the Quill plucks the string. This diagram will explain it—

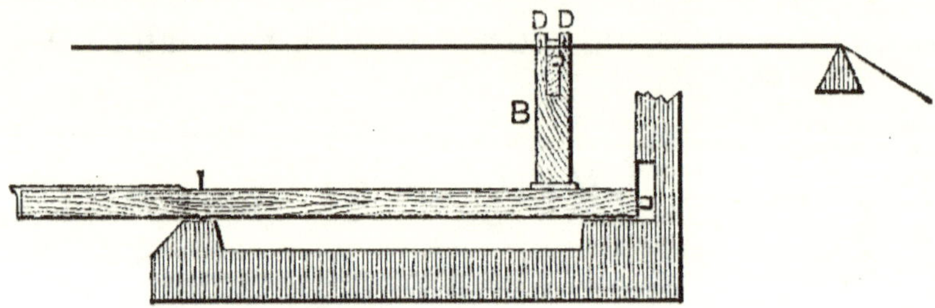

You see there the Key, do you not? And at the back of the Key you see the Jack (*B*). And at the top of the Jack you see the little projecting Quill, just ready to pluck the string. And you can see that if any one pressed down the Key the Jack would rise and the Quill would pluck, and the String would give forth its sound. That explains to you the Harpsichord. It is like a Zither, with a lot of strings of different lengths (long for low, and short for high). But unlike a Zither it has Keys and Jacks.

Some of the later Harpsichords had two or three strings for every note (so as to make a louder sound) and some had two keyboards (like the one in the plate), each with its own set of strings, just as a two-manual Organ has two keyboards, each with its own set of pipes. Some of the two-manual Harpsichords had a number of stops, which varied the sound in different ways (look once more at the plate). A simple Harpsichord, without such contrivances as these was sometimes called the **Virginals**, and sometimes the **Spinet**. Some people say the word 'Virginals' was applied to the instrument because it was played by the Virgin Queen—Elizabeth.

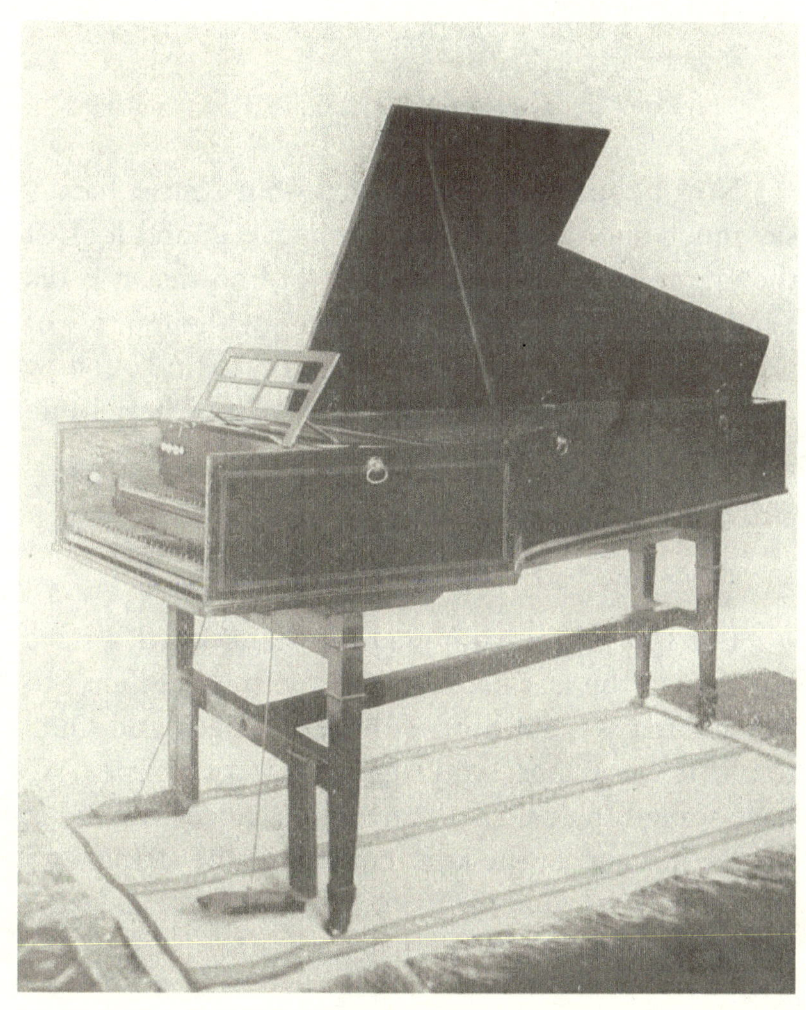

HARPSICHORD

But that explanation won't answer, for it was called the Virginals before she was born. As for the Spinet, the derivation of that word is easy enough—is not the string plucked by a spine?

The Pianoforte

Now about the PIANOFORTE—but I need hardly say much about that at this moment. Go and look at the one in your house and you will find that it is (as I called it) a Mechanical Dulcimer—with all kinds of wonderful modern improvements. Try to find out how it works. Then, later in the chapter, you shall have some pictures to help you.

The Clavichord

But I have not explained the Clavichord! I have left that to the last because it is the most difficult to explain. In the Clavichord we have not a Jack-and-Quill to pluck the strings. And we have not a Hammer. We have something called a Tangent—a piece of metal at the farther end of the key, that strikes the string, and then *stays stretching the string* as long as you leave the key down. Here is a diagram—

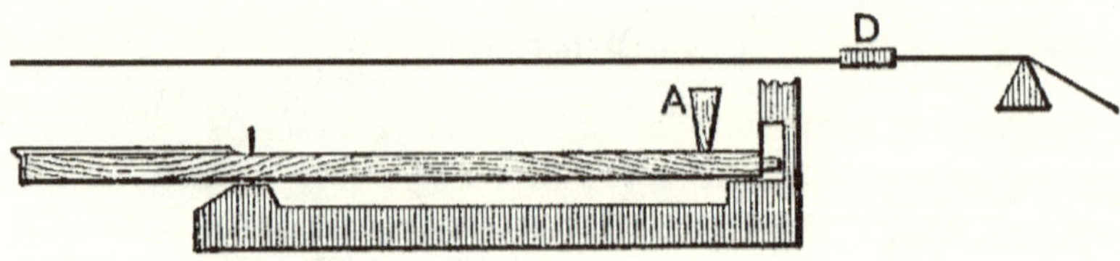

A is the Tangent, D is a bit of felt. When A strikes the string (and stays there, as I just told you) the longer end of the string sounds its note. Why does not the shorter end sound also? Because of that piece of felt, which 'damps' (as we say) that end of the string, or, in other words, checks its vibrations.

Whereas in the Harpsichord and Piano the whole string sounds, in the Clavichord the proper length of string for the note needed is, so to speak, 'cut off' by the Tangent. Sometimes, in early Clavichords, two keys next to one another would share the same string. Then of course the Tangent of the higher key cut off a shorter length than the Tangent of the lower string. For, as we have already learnt, higher notes come from shorter strings and lower notes from longer strings.

Of course, when two keys had only one string you could not play these two keys together.

What These Instruments Sound Like

The **Clavichord** is a very gentle instrument. It is suitable for small rooms, not for big concert-halls. Its sound has a lovely silvery quality. Bach wrote his famous forty-eight Preludes and Fugues for the Clavichord, and on that instrument they sound much more beautiful than on the Pianoforte. There is one special peculiarity about the Clavichord—by slightly moving your finger on the key you can keep a string in vibration, and so prolong the sound. The Clavichord cannot play loudly, but it can make very delicate shades of sound—louder and softer by small degrees.

The **Harpsichord** can, of course, play more loudly than the Clavichord. And if there are two manuals and some stops the player can get a lot of variety. But he cannot prolong the sound as a Clavichord player can, because once a string is plucked it *is* plucked, and there's an end of the matter. Moreover, the player cannot vary the loudness or softness of the sound much, excepting by using the stops, so the Harpsichordist cannot produce delicate *crescendos* and *diminuendos* and neat little accents, as the Clavichordist can.

As for the **Pianoforte**, you know what that sounds like. You cannot prolong the sound of it as you can that of the Clavichord, but (especially by using the sustaining pedal) you can make the sound last a good long while. And you can accent the notes, and make *crescendos* and *diminuendos* just as much as you like. Because this instrument, unlike the Harpsichord, could produce loud or soft notes at the player's will, it was called the 'Piano-Forte' (Italian for 'Soft-Loud'). Some photographs of the 'action' of a modern Piano are given a few pages later. When you have finished reading this chapter you should study them carefully.

Who Used These Instruments, and When

The first of these instruments to be invented was probably the **Clavichord**.

Then came the **Harpsichord**, so now both instruments were living side by side.

Then came the **Pianoforte**, so now there were three.

Then the **Clavichord** died out, so there were only two again.

And then the **Harpsichord** died out, so only the Pianoforte was left.

Nowadays, as I have said, people are reviving the Clavichord and Harpsichord. This is a good thing; they ought never to have been allowed to die!

The keyboard music of our Elizabethan composers (Byrd, Bull, Gibbons, Farnaby) was written for the early, simple Harpsichord, i.e. the **Virginals**.

The keyboard music of Purcell was also written for the Virginals.

The keyboard music of Bach was some of it written for the Clavichord and some of it for the Harpsichord. The Clavichord was Bach's favourite instrument. Some early pianos were shown to him by Frederick the Great, but he would not have them 'at any price' (of course, they were nothing like so good as our pianos to-day).

Handel's keyboard music (do you play the so-called *Harmonious Blacksmith*?) was written for the Harpsichord.

Mozart's keyboard music was also written for the Harpsichord, though possibly he played some of the later pieces on the Pianoforte.

Beethoven's keyboard music was written for the Pianoforte, and so was that of all the composers who followed him, for by this time Harpsichords were dying out, and Clavichords were practically already dead. But Beethoven never heard a Piano with such full loud tone as our Pianos to-day have. His was a gentler instrument than ours.

In Bach's day and Handel's day there was a Harpsichord in the Orchestra, and the conductor, instead of using a stick to direct the players, sat at the Harpsichord and led the band by playing with them.

Queen Elizabeth as a Player on the Virginals

Here is a story told by the Ambassador sent by Queen Mary of Scotland to the court of Queen Elizabeth of England:

> 'After dinner my lord of Hunsdean drew me up to a quiet gallery that I might hear some music (but he said that he durst not avow it), where I might hear the Queen play upon the virginals. After I had hearkened awhile, I took by the tapestry that hung before the door of the chamber, and seeing her back was toward the door, I entered within the chamber, and stood a pretty space hearing her play excellently well. But she left off immediately as soon as she turned about and saw me. She appeared to be surprised to see me, and came forward, seeming to strike me with her hand; alleging she used not to play before men, but when she was solitary, to shun melancholy. She asked how I came there. I answered, as I was walking with my lord of Hunsdean, as we passed by the chamber door, I heard such melody as ravished me, whereby I was drawn in ere I knew how; excusing my fault of homeliness, as being brought up in the court of France, where such freedom was allowed; declaring myself willing to endure what punishment her Majesty should be pleased to inflict upon me for so great an offence. Then she sat down

> low upon a cushion, and I on my knees beside her; but with her own hand she gave me a cushion to lay under my knee; which at first I refused, but she compelled me to take it. She then called for my Lady Strafford out of the next chamber; for the Queen was alone. She enquired whether my Queen or she played best. In that I found myself obliged to give her the praise.'

So wrote the Scottish Ambassador at the English court, and if you ask me I think that our vain Virginal-playing Queen had herself given Lord Hunsdean the hint to bring the Ambassador to hear her.

QUESTIONS

(To See Whether You Remember the Chapter and Understand It)

1. Describe how the sound is made in a Harpsichord.

2. Describe how the sound is made in a Pianoforte.

3. Describe how the sound is made in a Clavichord.

4. Which instrument did we call Mechanical Zither, and why?

5. And which did we call a Mechanical Dulcimer, and why?

6. What is a 'Virginal' (or 'Virginals'—the same thing)?

7. What is a Jack? Which instrument has Jacks?

8. What is a Tangent? Which instrument has Tangents?

THE ACTION OF A MODERN PIANO

These photographs show the mechanism of a single note taken out of an upright Piano, and so arranged as to make the movements clear to you.

You will see that a short brass rod has been placed in position to represent the piano string.

You will realize that there are two actions to be brought about by one mechanism—*(a)* the striking of the note, and *(b)* the silencing of it when the time comes for it to cease. This silencing we call 'Damping'.

You will notice, then, that the apparatus includes both a Hammer, to make the string sound, and a 'Damper', to stop its sounding.

When you put a key of the Piano down, the Damper comes away from the String (leaving it free to sound) and the Hammer strikes it (making it sound).

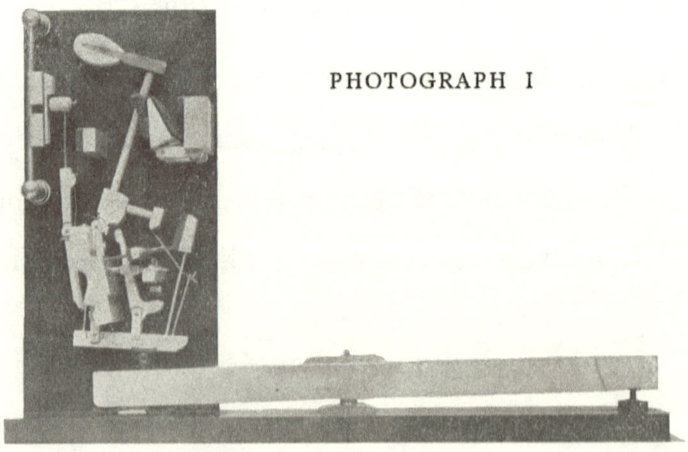

PHOTOGRAPH I

The player is beginning to press down the Key. The Hammer has begun to move forward towards the String. The Damper has not yet raised itself from the String.

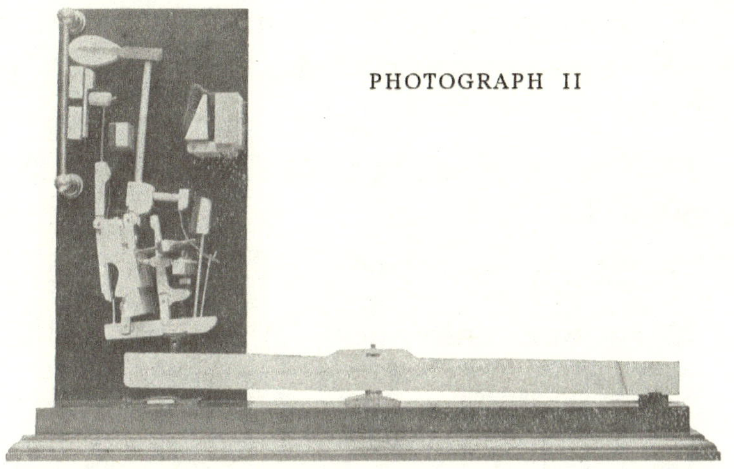

PHOTOGRAPH II

The Hammer is just in the act of striking the String and the Damper is raised from the String (look closely, and compare with Photograph I), and is thus allowing it to sound.

Of course, if the Hammer after striking remained touching the String, it would itself act as a 'Damper', and we should get very little sound. So, immediately after striking, it is made, by an ingenious arrangement, to fall back, out of the way.

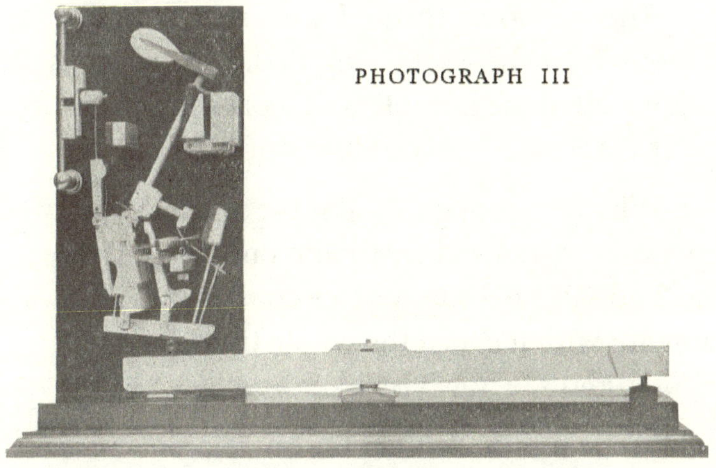

PHOTOGRAPH III

The player has removed his finger from the Key, the Damper has pressed forward and stopped the vibration of the String, and the Hammer has fallen back to its position of rest.

9. If you were giving a recital in a large Hall which would be the worst instrument for your purpose? And which the best?

10. Which was the first of the three instruments to be invented?

11. And which the last?

12. For which instrument did Byrd and Bull and Farnaby write?

13. And for which Bach?

14. And for which Handel?

15. And for which Mozart?

16. And for which Beethoven?

THINGS TO DO

1. There is one thing I never told you in the Chapter—how the Sustaining Pedal (sometimes, but wrongly, called the Loud Pedal) works. Open the front of your Piano and find out for yourself.

2. Why is it wrong to call it the Loud Pedal? Make a few experiments and try to find out. For instance, if it is the 'Loud Pedal' I suppose we could play a loud verse of a hymn with it down the whole time. Do this, listen carefully, and see how you like the effect.

3. Write a little Article for an imaginary musical magazine (or for your own school magazine, if you have one) on 'How the Piano Works'.

In the course of your article mention the predecessors of the Piano, and state the particular characteristics of each. State why the Piano's name in full is '*Pianoforte*'.

4. Write another Article on 'THE DIFFERENCES BETWEEN A PIANO AND AN ORGAN'.

5. For fun—ask the next six people you meet, 'What is the difference between a Piano Pedal and an Organ Pedal?' They are to answer straight away, without any time to think. Tell them it is not a riddle, but just a test of ordinary decent intelligence and observation.

THE FORTUNE THEATRE

CHAPTER VI

SHAKESPEARE THE MUSICIAN

If any of the learned Shakespeare writers should take up this book they will smile when they see the title of the present chapter, and say that they wonder how I know something about Shakespeare of which they never heard. So I must tell you how I know it.

Some people think that 'musician' means a man or woman who can play the piano or violin, or sing a song very beautifully, but I think that if any one has a musical ear, so that he *loves* music and understands it, then we may say that that person is a musician. Indeed I know people who have never learnt to sing or play at all, and yet are better musicians than some others who *can* do these things.

Now if there is one thing we can be quite sure about concerning Shakespeare, it is this—he had a musical ear and loved and understood music. I am going to prove that to you, and when you have read my proof you will be able to say with me, 'Yes; Shakespeare *was* a Musician.'

Shakespeare's Word-Music

You can tell that Shakespeare had a musical ear by reading his poetry, for when you do so you find that his words and lines are very musical. In a sense every poet must be a musician, for he has to choose beautiful, sweet-sounding words (that is—musical words), and arrange them so that they sound well with each other, just as the notes of a good tune sound well with each other. And then, too, he has to put them together in rhythm, just as a composer does with the notes of his tunes. If you take a line of the poetry of Shakespeare, or some other poet, you will find that it has accented syllables, just like a piece of music, so that you can divide it by bars if you like, as we do in the case of music. Shakespeare's lines generally have five bars. Just look at any blank verse passage of Shakespeare for a moment, and then try to put the bars in.

Then if you will look closely at any one of Shakespeare's most beautiful passages you will find that he has taken care to bring together sounds that fit one another, just as a musical composer brings together notes that fit. Let me give you just a few examples, and then, if you want, you can find thousands more for yourself. Often the musical effect is got by alliteration—that is the repetition of a letter-sound. For instance:

'pale primrose'

(p's)

'fierce fires'

(f's, r's, and s's)

'curled clouds'

(c's, d's, and l's)

'mischiefs manifold'

(m's and f's)

And you will find that sort of word-music on every page of Shakespeare.

Then we get a line such as:

'I will not struggle, I will stand stone still,'

with its st's and l's and n's;

or this:

'Whatever torment you may put me to,'

with its five t's and three m's;

or:

'Can sleep as soundly as the wretched slave,'

with its s's;

or:

'Then love-devouring death do what he dare,'

with its d's;

or:

'Stand tiptoe on the misty mountain tops,'

with its combination of m's, t's, and p's;

or:

'When the sweet wind did gently kiss the trees,'

with a combination of w's, d's, t's, and of s's, which, besides sounding pleasantly on our ears, seem to give us the very sound of the fluttered leaves;

or:

'Full fathom five thy father lies,'

nearly all f's and th's (two similar sounds), with l's to begin and end it.

Shakespeare's Word Discords

Sometimes Shakespeare seems to have chosen his consonants deliberately to suit the sentiment he wishes to express in his words. For instance there is this passage, where Juliet expresses her dislike of the lark's song, because it brings the unwelcome daybreak, and imagines in her dislike that the song is harsh and unpleasant:

It is the lark that sings so out of tune,
Straining harsh discords and unpleasing sharps.
Some say the lark makes sweet division;
This doth not so, for she divideth us:
Some say the lark and loathed toad change eyes.

There are more than twenty hissing s's in that short passage, and their use by the poet is almost like the use by a composer of the particular instrument, perhaps a harsh one, which he feels will best express the emotion he is at the moment trying to reproduce. This, then, is a sort of verbal orchestration.

Then what a variety of orchestration Shakespeare gets in a passage like this:

Strange and several noises
Of roaring, shrieking, howling, jingling chains.

Every word here reproduces a sound. Hear a really good actor say that, and you will realize that 'roaring' is like a blast of Trombones and Trumpets, 'shrieking' has high, loud Piccolo notes in it, 'howling' has String chromatic passages rising and falling rapidly, 'jingling' has something of Triangle and Cymbals.

Shakespeare's Vowel Music

So far I have been talking chiefly of Shakespeare's consonants. But if we examined his vowels we should find much the same thing. For instance:

and rifted Jove's stout oak
With his own bolt.

Look at those i's and o's.

Set out in musical fashion (Tonic-sol-fa-wise) this would be:

ă |ĭ :ĕ |ō :ow |ō : ‖ :ĭ |ĭ :ō |ō : ‖

or in Staff notation:

Say that over in the proper rhythm a few times and you will realize that there is a sort of vowel-rhyming patter in it, which is very agreeable to a musical ear.

Shakespeare's Rhythms

Now another word about rhythms. Many actors (most, I fear) spoil Shakespeare by destroying his rhythm. Very often, in trying to speak the lines expressively, they turn them from poetry into prose. When Shakespeare wants prose he writes prose, and when he sets his lines out as poetry he wants them to be read and recited as poetry. If you want to know how to recite Shakespeare, do as I just suggested—take a few lines of his and set them out with bars, as if they were music.

Let us take the line:

'Methought the billows spoke and told me of it';

set out in the Sol-fa tune notation that would be:

Me - | thought the | bil - lows | spoke and | told me | of it ||

la | la :la | la la :– | la :la | la :la | la la ||

or in Staff notation:

Me - | thought the | bil - lows | spoke and | told me | of it ||

Feel the Rhythm!

The lesson of this is that in reciting Shakespeare (or even in reading it to ourselves silently) we must feel the rhythm. Even a little child's jog-trot way of saying poetry is better than a grown-up person's would-be-clever way of reciting it 'expressively'. Of course it should be expressively recited, but the expression must not be allowed to kill the rhythm. Poetry comes between prose and music. It has words and thoughts, like prose, and it has rhythm and sound like music. And the more we can both grasp the thoughts and feel the rhythms and sound-patterns of Shakespeare the better we shall read and recite him and the more we shall enjoy him.

A great many people when they read Shakespeare lose all the musical side of his work. They are so busy studying his wonderful dramatic plots and his character-painting that they forget that there is also something to study in his use of sounds and his rhythms. If you like you can read a Shakespeare play merely as a tale, and you will get a great deal of pleasure. But if you look upon it as also a sort of Word-Symphony your pleasure will be increased. And as long as you live you can go on finding fresh musical beauties in Shakespeare.

Could Shakespeare Play or Sing?

But besides being a great 'word-musician' (one of the greatest there has ever been) it is quite likely that

Shakespeare was a player and singer. As you know from *The First Book of the Great Musicians*, in the days when he lived Englishmen and Englishwomen were famous for their playing of various instruments, and almost all of them could sing.

People were so musical that in a barber's shop there was often an instrument called a cittern (a kind of lute or guitar) hanging on the wall for any customer who was waiting his turn to be shaved to play upon, just as nowadays there are newspapers for him to read. So that shows that people *must* have been very musical in those days, doesn't it?

Some of the Instruments

There were other instruments, too, that people were very fond of (though they did not play these in barbers' shops), such as:

1. *The Virginals*: Something like a small grand piano in shape, and with a keyboard like a piano. Described in Chapter V.

2. *Viols*: A family of stringed instruments (little and big), something like our Violins, Violas, Violoncellos, and Double-basses.

3. *Lutes*: Another family of stringed instruments, but plucked, not bowed—something like the Mandoline of to-day, but better.

4. *Recorders*: A family of Flutes, blown at the end (not the side)—like tin whistles made of wood and very much glorified.

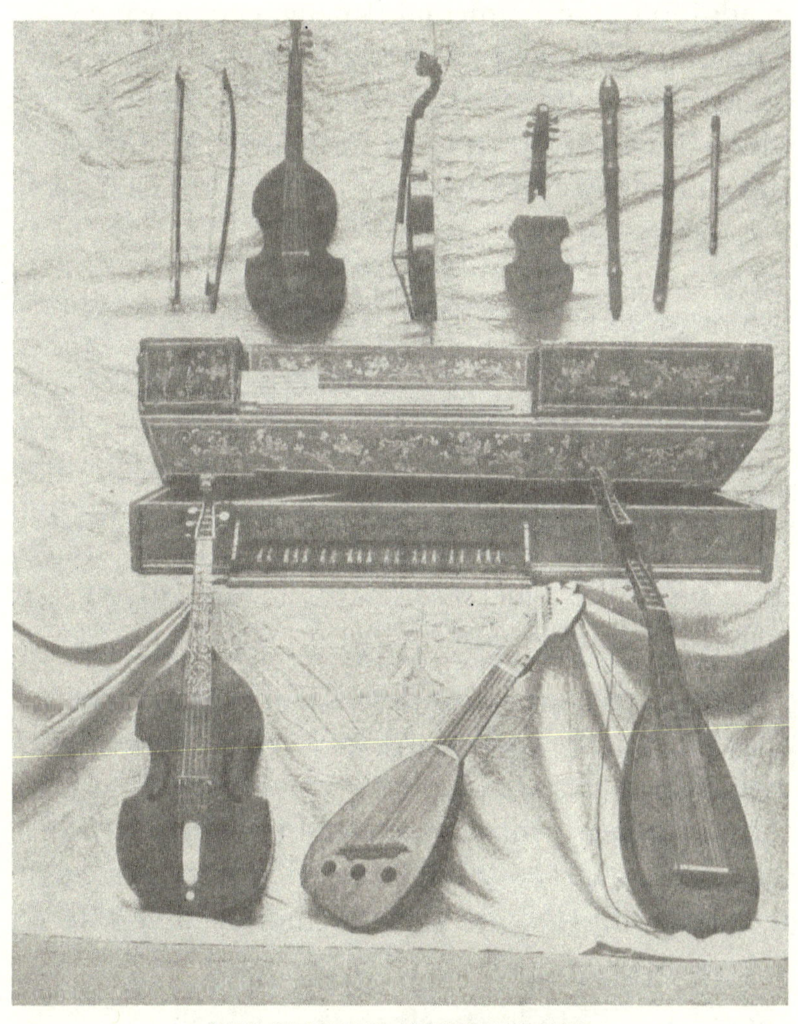

OLD ENGLISH INSTRUMENTS

Top Row: *Modern Bow and old Bow (showing difference in shape), Tenor Viol, Treble Viol, Small Treble Viol, Recorder, 'Cornet', Tabor Pipe*

Middle Row: *Queen Elizabeth's Virginal*

Bottom Row: *Viol da Gamba, two Lutes*

Shakespeare mentions all these instruments in his plays. In addition to instrumental playing, people were very fond of singing, and loved Madrigals (a sort of part-songs) and Rounds and Catches (like 'Three blind mice', which has come down to us from Shakespeare's day). This Choral Music has been spoken of in *The First Book.*

Shakespeare's Musical Plays

Now I come to something *very* important—the actual music that Shakespeare put into his plays. There is one point about this that even the learned Shakespeare writers have never discovered, but you and I, as musicians, can see it quite well if we look through the plays. *When Shakespeare wants to make us feel very awe-struck he uses music.*

You know that there are lots of ghosts and witches and fairies in the plays, don't you? Well, almost always when these strange, supernatural creatures appear there is music—sometimes singing and sometimes instruments. Get your English teacher to look through the plays with you, and you will find that this is so.

And then, too, when Shakespeare makes his characters fall in love, which, as you will some day find (but not too soon, I hope), is a very awe-inspiring, though happy, state to be in, he has music. When he represents anything that seems miraculous, such as people who seem to be dead restored to life, he has music again. And when real, actual death takes place (and this is the most awe-inspiring experience of all, isn't it?) then he often has music, too, so that one may be made to realize how solemn it all is, and feel touched by the sadness of it.

SHAKESPEARE'S DRAMATIC USE OF MUSIC

Some Illustrations of the Foregoing Chapter

Here are a few examples of Shakespeare's use of music. I have chosen them so that if you are reading any particular play of Shakespeare's you may find here a hint as to the purpose of the music in it. You need not read all that follows. It is just put into this book for you to refer to whenever you find it of interest to do so. Indeed this list of examples is perhaps more for the use of your English literature teacher than of yourself. If you are reading a Shakespeare play that is mentioned here, show this list to your teacher, and ask him or her to explain it.

Shakespeare's Fairies and Their Music

A Midsummer-Night's Dream. (1) Here we have the scene of a fairy queen and her court at their good-night revels—a picture in gossamer. Titania calls to her attendant fairies to sing her to sleep, and they join in the lovely song, 'You spotted snakes', with its soothing 'Lullaby' refrain.

(2) The fairy king and queen, Oberon and Titania, dance to music 'such as charmeth sleep', whilst the

spell is removed from the mortals who have passed so strange and disturbing a night in the 'Wood near Athens'.

(3) The play ends in the glimmering firelight, the happy lovers now retired to their several rooms receiving a blessing of song and dance as the fairies trip from room to room.

Music and Witchcraft

The witches of *Macbeth* have their own grim music. (1) Hecate, the Queen of the Witches, is summoned in music ('*Music and a Song within: "Come Away"*'). The use of music behind the scenes, mysterious music from we know not whither, is plainly Shakespeare's way of impressing us with a sense of weirdness and mystery.

(2) When the cavern and cauldron scene is reached, shortly after, we find music again; at Hecate's command the witches sing ('*Music and a Song: "Black Spirits"*'). Macbeth appears, and for him they conjure up the three apparitions, each with thunder. At last the cauldron sinks—to music (the rough, coarse tone of early seventeenth-century hautboys is the music Shakespeare calls for in his directions). Then the witches dance to music—and vanish.

Ghostly Music

Cymbeline. Posthumus is in prison. He sleeps, and 'Solemn music' is heard. Then pass before the dreamer in procession, his father and mother, with musicians walking before them and after them followed by his brothers, 'with wounds, as they died in the wars'. Once again, Shakespeare has contrived to awaken in his audience a sense of the uncanny, and, again, largely by music.

Antony and Cleopatra. It is night. Four soldiers are on guard before the palace. Suddenly, as they talk in undertones of the battle of the morrow, music is heard, coming from nowhere (Shakespeare's directions are '*Music of hautboys as under the stage*'). Awestruck, the sentinels speculate as to its meaning. The music moves away, and they follow it. Here again (this time acting on a hint from Plutarch) the dramatist has used music to produce an impressive effect; into our minds, by the music and the anxious conversation of the soldiers about it is brought the strained feeling of the eve of battle.

Julius Caesar. Brutus is in his tent. The great quarrel with Cassius has just occurred, and the moving reconciliation has followed. The friends have now parted for the night, and Brutus feels the need of calm. He asks his boy, 'Where is thy instrument?' The sleepy boy plays, and drops asleep as he does so. Quieted in mind Brutus takes up a book to read, when Caesar's ghost enters. Here, again, music has tuned the minds of the audience and prepared them for great happenings. A stage ghost, unheralded by music, is little likely to be convincing to an audience, though once, in Hamlet, Shakespeare has achieved ghostly conviction by other than musical means.

The Winter's Tale. The King has, he believes, killed his Queen. Long years after, when he has become repentant and mourns his ill-doing, he is invited to see a statue of the murdered Queen. Then, as he gazes, the word is given, music strikes on his ear, and to it the statue comes slowly to life, steps down from its pedestal and embraces him—no statue, indeed, but his actual wife, long hidden from him by some who loved her. It is to music that an apparent miracle takes place—without music perhaps to most of us no miracle but a commonplace conjuring trick. Music and the sense of mystery are once more associated.

Henry VIII. A case like that of Posthumus, already quoted, is the one of poor, ill-used Queen Katharine. 'Take thy lute, wench,' she says, 'my soul grows sad with troubles. Sing and disperse 'em.' Then comes the lovely song, 'Orpheus with his lute'. Later in the play the Queen again calls for musical comfort, and this time, in vision, 'spirits of peace' appear to her. The audience is brought to realize that the Queen is already in touch with that spiritual kingdom to which she is so soon to pass. (Not all of this play is by Shakespeare himself, but, musically, his principles are followed.)

Music and the Act of Choice

The Merchant of Venice. Bassanio's choice, on which his life's happiness and that of the woman he loves depend, is made to music ('*Music whilst Bassanio comments on the caskets to himself*'). For the previous suitors Shakespeare provided no music, but here, in the case of Bassanio, is a choice on which turns the whole plot of the play, and the dramatist uses a musical means to bring the solemnity of it home to us. The point cannot be laboured here, but is there not something of the supernatural about the act of choosing; do we not feel a sense of mystery when pondering a great decision?

Music as Medicine

You are not likely to read *Pericles* just at present, as it is not a play of much interest to younger people. But when you are older you will probably do so and then you may be interested to refer to what follows:

(1) Thaisa, wife of Pericles, travelling with him by sea, gives birth to a child during a storm, and, as is thought, dies. Her body is hastily placed in a large chest and cast over into the sea. The chest floats ashore, and is carried to Cerimon, a lord of the place, by his servants. The body is discovered, and Cerimon announces that life is not extinct. He calls for fire, clothes, and appliances and—for music. To the sound of the viol the Queen is restored to conscious life. Dramatically the case is interesting. The use of drugs would have been prosaic and commonplace; extraordinary means are used for the performance of what is almost a miracle, and the attention and awe of the audience are secured.

(2) Heartbroken at the loss of his wife, Pericles soon suffers another loss—his daughter, the babe born on shipboard, being carried away by pirates. Years after,

distraught by sorrow, he comes to Mytilene, lying speechless in a pavilion on the deck of his ship. The Governor of the place comes off to see him, and to the attendants proposes, as a cure, the music of a maid famous for such in Mytilene. She is sent for. No immediate cure is effected, but the music was not without effect, for, on her speaking to the stricken prince, he replies. A gradual recovery takes place, and Pericles recognizes in the music-maid his lost daughter. Then mysterious music in the air steals into his ears and ours; to it he drops into a calm slumber, during which, to music, Diana appears to him and proclaims to him the impending recovery of his wife. The plot of *Pericles* is, in fact, the separation of a family by storm and violence and its re-union by music. There is very slight exaggeration in this statement.

King Lear. Cordelia sits in the camp beside her poor old mad father. He sleeps, 'soft music playing'; the latter provided by the doctor's orders as a means of restoring shattered nerves and shaken mental powers. Lear wakes, bewildered and hardly able to realize he is still on earth. Gradually he collects his mental forces and recovery is evident. (Compare the prescription of Saul's servants, in *his* madness.)

Music as a Sign of Madness

Snatches of song, abrupt and disorganized, are with Shakespeare one of the symptoms of madness, as ordered organized music is its cure. Lear 'singing aloud; Crowned with rank fumiter and furrow weeds', and Hamlet's Ophelia, again with song and flowers, are cases in point.

Those of Shakespeare's characters who feign a lack of wit, his clowns and fools, show the same sign of irresponsibility—the clown in *Twelfth Night* visiting Malvolio in prison, Edgar in *King Lear* 'disguised as a Madman', and calling himself Poor Tom, are amongst the examples.

Petruchio, in *The Taming of the Shrew*, pretends to be a man of uncontrolled impulse, so that he may subdue his violent wife—and it is part of his pretence that he sings mad snatches of wild melody.

As to the state of drunkenness, surely akin to that of madness, the references to this in the above must suffice for the moment.

Love and Music

Romeo calls on Juliet—'If the measure of thy joy be heaped like mine . . . then sweeten with thy breath the neighbour air, and let rich music's tongue unfold the imagined happiness'. The Duke in *Twelfth Night*, in whom music is 'the food of love', is, however, Shakespeare's greatest instance of the lover who needs music. Cleopatra, in *Antony and Cleopatra*, calls for 'some music, moody food of us that trade in love', and even when she goes a-fishing has her 'music playing far off'. Don Adriano, in *Love's Labour's Lost*, is another musical lover ('Sing, boy; my spirit grows heavy in love', and, later, 'Warble, child; make passionate my sense of hearing '). Speed, in *Two Gentlemen of Verona*, speaks of one of the signs of love—'To relish a love-song like a robin-redbreast'. Claudio in *Much Ado about Nothing*, having become a lover, becomes a devotee of the tabor and pipe.

The love-serenades in *Two Gentlemen of Verona*, and *Cymbeline*, and elsewhere, and the many references to such in other plays must pass with mere allusion.

In *The Merchant of Venice*, Shakespeare has cunningly used music and moonlight (and romantic conversation about both of them) to bring our hearts into tune with those of the three newly and happily married couples.

Music and Death

Music is heard to prepare us for the death of Richard II, and Henry IV ('Let there be no noise made, my gentle friends; unless some dull and favourable hand will whisper music to my weary spirit'). King John sings as he lies a-dying. Desdemona chants her sad songs as the shadow of impending death creeps over the stage. Claudio, in *Much Ado*, sings at the grave of his betrothed.

Hamlet and *Coriolanus* end with dead marches. So does *King Lear*. In these plays, the spirit of tragedy reaches its culmination in music. But the most touching instance of the connexion of music and death is in the harping and singing over the body of Imogen, in *Cymbeline* ('Fear no more the heat of the sun').

Music in 'The Tempest'

The unfolding of the plot in *The Tempest* almost turns on music. Yet many otherwise excellent critical essays have been written on the play, without so much as a mention of music.

In *The Tempest* every one is musical—the human beings, the fairy-sprite, Ariel, and the man-devil, Caliban. Music, throughout the play, is the means by which the actions of mortals are directed. To treat this subject at all adequately would mean at least two pages. Read *The Tempest* for yourself, marking the instances where music is heard or spoken of, and then consider why Shakespeare made of this a musical play.

QUESTIONS

(To See Whether You Remember the Chapter and Understand It)

1. What is a musician?

2. Are you one?

3. Do you, or do you not, agree with me that Shakespeare was a *Word-Musician*?

4. And (in either case) why?

5. Why do we think Shakespeare may have been a player or singer (or both)?

6. Mention a few of the instruments Shakespeare must often have heard.

7. Why did Shakespeare use so much music in his plays?

THINGS TO DO

1. Turn to your favourite passage of Shakespeare and see whether there is any 'Consonant Music' in it.

2. And whether there is any 'Vowel Music'.

3. Pick up one or two of the best lines and say them over a good many times until you feel sure you've seized the rhythm.

4. Then write down this music rhythmically (in either Staff notation or Sol-fa *la's*), and write the words under the music.

5. If you are reading a Shakespeare play at school, go through it and make a list of any references to music.

6. Then write a little essay on 'Shakespeare's Use of Music in *The Tempest*' (or whatever the play may be).

7. If there is a musical part of this play, that can be acted conveniently, act it with some of your school friends.

8. There is one sort of music in Shakespeare that the chapter never mentions. What is it? . . . *Quite right!* The ceremonial music—Trumpets when great personages enter, Hautboys and other instruments when soldiers march, etc. Now see if you can find a few examples of that.

CHAPTER VII

MORE ABOUT BRITISH MUSIC

If you look back over the two parts of *The Book of the Great Musicians* that came before this one you will find that I have hardly seemed to be quite fair to British Music. The only chapters, so far, on British Composers have been:

1. 'English Music in the Days of Drake and Shakespeare'.

2. 'Henry Purcell—the Greatest British Composer'.

3. 'The Inventor of the Nocturne—John Field'.

4. 'Edward Elgar'.

Let us set out in centuries all the British names so far mentioned:

Sixteenth Century

Tallis, Byrd, Bull, Gibbons, Farnaby, Dowland, and others (nearly all these lived on into the next century).

Seventeenth Century

Henry Purcell.

EIGHTEENTH CENTURY

Field (lived into the next century).

NINETEENTH CENTURY

Elgar (still alive in next century).
Sullivan.

A Comparison with Germany

Now suppose we make a list of the great German and Austrian Composers who were living and working during the eighteenth and nineteenth centuries:

EIGHTEENTH CENTURY

Bach (born previous century).
Handel (born previous century).
Haydn (lived into next century).
Mozart.
Beethoven (lived into next century).
Schubert (lived into next century).
Weber (lived into next century).

NINETEENTH CENTURY

Mendelssohn.
Schumann.
Wagner.
Brahms.

I could have made a longer list of German Composers if I had wished, but I thought it best only to include the very greatest, yet even so you will at once get the idea that during the eighteenth and nineteenth centuries Germany went far ahead of Britain in music, and this idea, I am sorry to say, is true.

How It Happened

Why did this happen? Different people give different reasons.

1. Some say it was because at the beginning of the century Handel came to this country, and was so great a composer that people did not wish to listen to our British composers unless they imitated Handel (and imitation is always a weak thing and never results in much).

2. Others say it was because the British were so busy fighting and exploring and trading that they had not time for music. But this does not seem to be a very good reason, for we were very actively fighting and exploring and trading in the sixteenth century, yet we had plenty of fine composers then.

3. Still others say it was because in Germany and Austria there were a great many different centres at which fine music was going on, whereas in Britain there was really not much going on except in London.

You can form your own ideas, but for myself I think there is something in 1 and 3, and, perhaps, especially in 3.

Centres of Musical Activity

I must explain to you a little this idea about the number of centres in Germany and Austria. The chief places where music was cultivated in the seventeenth and eighteenth centuries were the Courts of monarchs. A King would have his private Orchestra, and often his private Opera House, and generally his Organist and Choir to carry out the music in the Royal Chapel, and lots of other music of different sorts.

For instance, Henry VIII and Queen Elizabeth had fine Royal Chapel choirs, and (as you have learnt) encouraged Masques (which are something like Operas), and also stimulated the playing of the Virginals and the composing of music for them by having about their Courts good players and composers who could provide them with entertainment. And Charles II, James II, and William and Mary continued this cultivation of music to some extent, their chief musician being, as you know, Purcell. But there were in Britain only two Courts in early times, and after the Stuarts came to the English throne only one, whereas what we now call Germany was then a number of separate small states, each with its own King, or Duke, or Elector to rule it, and, thus, each with its own Court, which generally had a Royal Choir for its Chapel, a Royal Orchestra, a Royal String Quartet, and a Royal Opera Company.

The Development of Instrumental Music

Now the time had come in the history of music when the great thing needed was the development of Instrumental Music and of the Opera. The eighteenth century is especially the century of the invention and perfection of the Sonata and the Symphony. But how could people in Britain compose Symphonies, when they had no decent orchestras except in London? You see what I mean: almost every Court in the German countries was a centre of musical enthusiasm and culture, and the British had only one centre, whereas these lands had a great many. So I think they can be forgiven.

What of To-day?

Nowadays, of course, things are rather different. Many towns have their Orchestras, and there are good Choral Societies everywhere, and public concerts, and good education in music. The British still concentrate their music too much in London, but nevertheless we may fairly say that the old conditions have disappeared, because in this and all countries fine music is no longer dependent on Courts and Kings, but has come right down to the people at large. And a very good thing too—since it gives us all a chance! And, of course, in America the same thing has happened.

Naturally, from Purcell to the present day there

have been English composers at work. But until recently they have not been great enough men to rank with those on the Continent.

This is just a short chapter to explain to you how it came about that Britain, which often took the lead so long as music was a matter of Choral Singing and Virginal Playing, fell behind when it became a matter of Opera performance and Orchestral Concerts. In a few short chapters which follow I shall tell you a little about some of the best of the British composers during this rather dull period, and also about some of the best during our own more vigorous days.

QUESTIONS

(To See Whether You Remember the Chapter and Understand It)

1. Mention all the British composers you can remember whose names have so far come into these three *Books of the Great Musicians.*

2. Give as clear an idea as you can of when they lived.

3. Mention all the German and Austrian composers discussed in the three parts of this book.

4. Give as clear an idea as you can of when they lived.

5. What are the three reasons sometimes given for Britain's falling behind?

6. Which do you yourself think are most likely to be true?

7. Why should a King or a Court have so much influence on music?

8. Tell anything you can about British monarchs and music.

9. What do we mean if we say 'Music is now a democratic art'? Is it true?

10. Is it wholly true?

11. Is it as true as it might be?

12. Have you any suggestions for making it more true?

THINGS TO DO

Think of some for yourself. I can't think of any except this—You might get up a good school concert called 'An Afternoon of British Music'. The programme would be something like this:

1. A piece or two of Elizabethan keyboard music, e.g. something of Farnaby (published by Novello).

2. A piece or two of Purcell's keyboard music (published by Chester).

3. A Purcell Song, by one of the Singing Classes.

4. One movement, or two movements, from Purcell's Violin Sonata (published both by Schott and by Curwen).

5. Another Purcell Song by another of the Singing Classes.

6. If you have a School Orchestra, one or two of Purcell's little pieces arranged for Strings (published by Novello).

7. An Arne Song by one of the Singing Classes (read about Arne in the next chapter).

8. A Field Nocturne by the best pianist in the school.

9. A Sullivan Song by one of the masters or mistresses or by some local singer who wants to help you (let it be a song from one of the Comic Operas—don't have *The Sailor's Grave* or *The Lost Chord*, which are very poor Sullivan).

10. Something of Elgar's if you can manage it.

11. To end the concert, *Elgar's Land of Hope and Glory* by the whole school, or Arne's *Rule, Britannia* (but don't let them sing 'Britannia rules the waves—which is wrong!), and then *God save the King.*

Another plan would be to get up a subscription to buy British records for the school Gramophone and then give a Gramophone Concert of Madrigals, Purcell, Arne, and Elgar. Or you could have *both* concerts with a month or so between them, perhaps raising money by the first in order to get the records to give the second—which might then be free.

I have just thought of another thing to do (I am assuming now that I am speaking to British readers; American readers are not so likely to want to do this). Write to the British Music Society, 3 Berners Street, W., and ask the Secretary how to form a School Branch of the Society.

CHAPTER VIII

ARNE, THE COMPOSER OF 'RULE, BRITANNIA'

1710-1778

THERE is at least one eighteenth-century British composer about whom you ought to know something; especially as you have certainly heard and probably sung some of his songs—Thomas Augustine Arne.

Arne was an Eton boy who made himself a nuisance to his school-fellows by practising on an old cracked flute, so that years after, when old Dr. Burney, who was writing his great *History of Music*, asked several of them to tell him about Arne's schooldays that was what they told him, and he duly put it into his 'History':

> 'I have been assured by several of his school-fellows that his love for music operated on him too powerfully, even while he was at Eton, for his own peace or that of his companions; for with a miserable cracked common flute, he used to torment them night and day, when not obliged to attend school.'

How the Boy Arne Went to the Opera

Then Burney asked Arne himself to tell him about his early life, and he told him how after he had left Eton he used to get into the Opera House without paying.

His father was an upholsterer and had a shop not very far from the Opera House. Now, in those days, whilst the masters and mistresses were in the stalls and boxes of the theatre, their servants, who had to wait for them either to drive them home again or to attend them on foot with torches, were allowed to sit in the gallery. So young Arne used to borrow the livery of a footman, put it on, walk boldly in at the gallery door and spend the evening enjoying the music.

You may be sure his father did not know of this, for he intended him to be a lawyer and did not encourage him to study music.

How He Practised the Harpsichord

You remember, from the first volume, how little Handel got over his difficulty by taking a harpsichord up to the garret and practising quietly at night, when the family was asleep. Well, Arne, as a youth, tried the same trick.

Perhaps Arne learnt this trick from Handel, for Handel was born twenty-five years before Arne, came to England in the very year of Arne's birth, and all through Arne's earlier life was the most popular composer in

THOMAS ARNE

England. No doubt Handel sometimes talked of his boyish escapades and the tales might come to Arne's ears. Handel, you remember, was found out, his harpsichord being heard one night by the family. Arne was more wary. He used to put a handkerchief over the strings in such a way as to muffle the sound.

Arne as a Lawyer

The part of London where Arne's father lived was (and is still) crowded with lawyer's offices, and Arne was sent to one of these to serve his 'articles', or apprenticeship.

Soon after the 'articles' were served, Mr. Arne, senior, had occasion one evening to call on a customer of his. He heard music and was told a private concert was being held, and was invited to go upstairs and become one of the audience. When he walked into the room what was his surprise to find that the leading violinist was his own son! 'Who taught you to play the fiddle?' he must have asked, and then young Tom had to confess that all the time he had been studying law he had been studying the fiddle too, taking lessons from a famous London fiddler of those days, called Festing.

Arne Teaches His Sister and Brother

The father saw that his boy was meant by nature to be a musician and not a lawyer, so he forgave him, and allowed him to practise music openly at home in future, and also to give lessons to his sister, who seemed to have a pretty good voice. So good, indeed, was her voice, and so well did he teach her that she was soon able to appear in public at the Opera House, and then, finding her a great success as an opera singer, Arne wrote an opera called *Rosamund* specially for her. His little brother appeared in this too, so it looks as though the father had quite got over any objection to his family taking part in music.

The opera was performed ten times, the last time for the benefit of the composer, who probably made a nice little sum of money that night. He was now twenty-three.

This success had to be followed up, of course, so Arne wrote another opera, on Tom Thumb, with his young brother in the part of the hero.

Arne Composes 'Rule, Britannia!'

Arne was now becoming quite well known and soon he was asked by many theatre managers to compose music for them. When he was thirty a great musical performance was to be given in the garden of the country house of the Prince of Wales, at Cliveden in Buckinghamshire. Arne was asked to write the music for a masque called *Alfred*, and did so. The song which ended the masque was one which soon became very well known—*Rule, Britannia!*

What are the next words after 'Rule, Britannia'? 'Britannia rules the waves.' There, I knew you'd say that.

And of course you're wrong, for if the poet were about to make the statement, 'Britannia rules the waves', he would not, just before this, tell her to do that very thing. The first bar of the chorus (from which the title of the song has been taken) is really 'Rule, Britannia! Britannia, *rule* the waves!' (imperative mood, not indicative).

Wagner, years after this song was written, heard it and said 'the first eight notes contain the whole character of the British people.'

Other Arne Songs

Other songs which have helped to make Arne famous are some that he wrote for a performance of Shakespeare's *As You Like It*:

1. 'Under the greenwood tree.'

2. 'Blow, blow, thou winter wind.'

3. 'When daisies pied.'

Later, for Shakespeare's *The Tempest*, he wrote another very beautiful song, which is often heard to-day:

4. 'Where the bee sucks.'

It is chiefly by his songs that we remember Arne to-day, for his Operas and Oratorios are forgotten. But the songs have such good *tunes* that they will, I should think, never die. A really good simple tune is one of the finest gifts to his countrymen a composer can leave behind him when he dies.

Besides solo vocal and choral music Arne wrote some harpsichord and violin music that is still worth playing.

Women in Oratorios

Now I have told you just enough about Arne to make you feel interested when you hear any of his music, and so to make you listen to it more carefully, which is what I meant to do. There is just one thing further I will tell you.

If you hear a Choral Society singing an Oratorio to-day, who sings the Treble and Alto parts? Ladies, of course! Well, until Arne thought of giving the ladies a chance to take part in Choral Singing (in his Oratorio *Judith*, in 1773) nobody had ever done so. They used, up to his day, to have boy Sopranos and men Altos, and no women at all. So all Handel's Oratorios were originally sung (except for some of the solo parts) entirely by boys and men.

The Influence of Folk Song

There is another thing I ought to tell you, or rather to which I ought to draw your attention. Arne's best songs are very *English* in melody. English Folk Song has had its influence on Arne, as you can feel. Now remember this:

1. Those Elizabethan composers I talked of in the first volume used a lot of English Folk Songs in their keyboard music—often making a long piece by taking a Folk Song and then writing Variations upon it.

2. Purcell's songs have often got the English Folk Song style about them.

3. Arne's songs have this too.

4. Sullivan's songs, in his comic operas, are often 'influenced' by English Folk Song.

5. Some composers to-day, like Vaughan Williams, have the English Folk Song influence in their music.

So you see that the Folk Songs of which we read in the very first chapter of *The First Book of the Great Musicians* have always had an influence upon English composers.

'Folk Music' and 'Art Music'

In another book I have put it this way—Folk Music is like the Wild Rose, which just grows up nobody knows how, and without any watering, or pruning, or tending of any kind. 'Art' Music (that is, real 'Composed' Music) is like the Garden Rose, which centuries of clever gardening have developed out of the Wild Rose.

And all the time that the Garden Rose has been developing the Wild Rose has gone on flourishing. And the two to-day still grow side by side—one on one side of the garden wall, and one on the other side.

In Purcell's and Arne's songs you see the Wild Rose gradually turning into the Garden Rose, but still not so very much unlike the Wild Rose. In some music to-day you see the Garden Rose so much developed that at first you are in danger of forgetting that it ever came from the Wild Rose. But so it was, and if you think about it for a moment you will see that every bit of 'Composed' Music is really the development of the Folk Music from which the first composers got their ideas about composition.

QUESTIONS

(To See Whether You Remember the Chapter and Understand It)

1. When was Arne born?

2. When did he die?

3. Where did he go to school?

4. For what profession was he trained when he left school?

5. And how did hc managc to cscapc from it?

6. What do you know of *(a)* Arne's Father, *(b)* his Sister, (c) his Brother?

7. Which branch of Arne's composition is best remembered to-day?

8. Mention any pieces by Arne.

9. What did Wagner say about *Rule, Britannia*?

10. What do you think about this saying?

11. What change in Oratorio performance did Arne bring about?

12. Repeat any ideas about Folk Song which you have got out of this Chapter.

THINGS TO DO

1. Get your singing-class teacher to teach you some Arne songs.

2. Persuade your Form to give a half-hour Form Concert of Music by Arne, and to admit the rest of the school.

3. Look through the Gramophone Record Catalogue for any pieces by Arne, and persuade your parents that it would add to the family happiness to have the ready means of performing such good tunes.

4. Ask your English Teacher to set as a subject for composition *The Life and Works of Arne*. And your French teacher to set you a brief French composition:

'Comment Arne assistait à l'Opéra sans payer', or

'Comment le jeune Arne devint musicien en dépit de son père'.

(If you want to know the French for 'upholsterer', it is *'tapissier'*; 'harpsichord' is *'clavecin'*; 'to muffle' is *assourdir'*—and now you're ready to start!)

CHAPTER IX

STERNDALE BENNETT

1816-1875

THE proverb says 'Give a dog a bad name and you may as well hang him.' The idea is, I suppose, that once you make people think that the dog is useless or vicious they will go on thinking so, and by and by he will think so himself, and then will probably actually become so, and so, in the end, deserve his fate.

In the same way, if there is a boy at school who is always being told he's a worthless scamp he will probably become more and more worthless all the time, whereas if he got a bit of encouragement now and again, when his better side came out, he would probably develop that better side, and in time become as good a scholar and as well behaved a one as his companions.

Of course we must not push this idea too far, but there is something in it. On the whole it is better to encourage than to blame.

The Depressed Britons

Now at the beginning of the nineteenth century the British composers did not get a great deal of encouragement. During the preceding century Germany (as we have seen in the last chapter but one) had had Bach and Handel, Haydn and Mozart, and now it had Beethoven and Weber and others. And Britain had no musical giants of that size. So British people came to have a poor idea of their own composers, and not to give them much encouragement to work hard and become greater, until soon there was an idea that Britain was not a music-producing country, although, if people had only stopped to think, they would have remembered the Elizabethans, and Purcell, and would have seen that even Arne, although not a great composer, was, on the whole, a quite good one.

How Mendelssohn Found a British Composer

The way a change of thought came about is rather interesting. There was a student at the Royal Academy of Music who was a good violinist and pianist and composer. Now one day Mendelssohn, who was visiting England, was invited to be present at a Students' Concert at the Academy. When he had heard this student play a Concerto of his own he said, 'I want to have a good look at that boy.' So they brought the boy and he was introduced, and Mendelssohn said, 'You must come to

WILLIAM STERNDALE BENNETT, AGED ABOUT 16

Germany.' The boy replied, 'If I come to Germany may I come as your pupil?' but Mendelssohn said 'No, no, you must come as my friend.'

This boy was William Sterndale Bennett, and he was then seventeen. He went to Germany a few years later, and Mendelssohn, Schumann, and other musicians there made much of him. So, when he came back, people in England thought more of him and listened more readily to his music, and put it into concert programmes. Germany was considered the great musical country then, and if the young composer was praised there the English people were prepared to believe in him.

The Turn of the Tide

So Sterndale Bennett got his chance. I may as well say at once that his life is a little disappointing to read because the promise of his youth was never *quite* fulfilled. He wrote a lot of fine things and then, in middle life, got so tied up with teaching work, on which in those days every musician in England had to depend for a living, that he stopped composing. But before he did so he had done one splendid thing—given the British people a bit of faith in their own composers. Bennett is the tide mark in British music. Before him the tide was always going out: after him it began to flow in again and to rise higher and higher, until now it has risen very high indeed (or so it seems to those of us to-day who are watching it).

A North Country Musical Family

Sterndale Bennett belonged to a North Country musical family. He was born at Sheffield, where his father was an Organist, and his grandfather a Singer and a player on the Oboe. When William was three his father died, and his grandfather, who was then living in Cambridge as a member of the choir of King's College, adopted him, brought him up, and when he was eight had him admitted as a choir-boy.

How Sterndale Bennett Went to London

When the boy was ten, as he seemed very gifted in music, he was sent to London to try if he could win a place in the new Royal Academy of Music. In those days the Academy was very different from what it is now. Small boys were accepted as students. They lived at the Academy itself, and they wore a uniform.

The examiners tested Bennett and were so pleased with him that they decided he should be admitted without paying any fees at all, which was a very unusual concession. His grandparents had expected that, even if successful, he would come back to Cambridge for a time, and had only given him the things necessary for one night, but he was told to start his residence at the Academy at once and sent to join the other boys who were already students.

The Boys' Ear-Test

One of the Professors went to another one and said, 'Come and see the funny little fellow who has just come into the house!' They went to the room where the boys were, and there was little Bennett being put through another examination, this time by the boys. They had put him in a corner of the room and were striking on the piano handfuls of notes, and asking him to name them, and he could do it correctly every time.

I think the boys liked this new companion all the better for being small, for they were able to let him down out of the window in a basket at night to go and buy good things to eat.

Bennett Becomes a 'Grand-Pupil' of Mozart and Beethoven

Bennett had a beautiful alto voice, and sometimes Mr. Attwood, the organist of St. Paul's, would send for him to sing in the choir. Attwood had been a pupil of Mozart, and Potter, who was Bennett's teacher, had been a pupil of Beethoven. So no doubt he would hear tales of these great composers. Later in his life he made Mozart's music his special study, and advised every one who wished to compose clearly to do the same.

At this time he did not often see his grandparents in Cambridge, and could not even write to them very often, for in those days postage was very costly, and was paid by the person who received the letter, and

Bennett's grandfather could not afford the fees that were charged. You will realize, if you think for a few minutes, that very few of the great musicians you have read about in *The First Book of the Great Musicians* or *The Second Book of the Great Musicians* came of well-to-do families, and some of them, as you see, were really poor in their boyhood. Bennett's main instrument at the Academy was the Violin, but after a time he was allowed to give more attention to the Piano. One fact that will surprise you is this—all the practice pianos of the Academy were in one room, and a number of pupils would practise together, all playing their different pieces at the same time. A retired sergeant was always in the room to see they did not neglect their work, and he must have suffered, poor man! But he used always to go and stand by Bennett's piano and listen to him, and perhaps he trained himself to keep the sounds of the others out of his head.

Bennett as Organist

When Bennett was eighteen, and already an accomplished musician who had been praised by Mendelssohn, there was a vacancy for an organist at a church at Wandsworth, and he decided to try for it. In those days the parishioners used to vote for their organist, and when they met there was a show of hands, and it was seen that Bennett had lost. But those who were in favour of his being given the post demanded a poll. This was held. The polling booth was open all day, just as in a Parliamentary Election nowadays, and when at night they counted the votes they found that Bennett had a majority of 67. So he got the post, and with it £30 a year as salary. But he was still very poor, and sometimes, in going to Wandsworth, had no money to pay the toll at the bridge over the river and would leave with the bridge-keeper his gloves, or some other little thing, instead of money. Soon, however, he began to get some pupils near London, and to make a little money in this way too. He still lived at the Academy, however, and was considered to be a student there.

Some Pianoforte Music

Possibly some of the readers of this book play Bennett's three pieces, *The Lake, The Mill Stream*, and *The Fountain*. These were written whilst he was still at the Academy, and when he was about twenty. His own playing of these became famous. Then he went to Germany (as I have already related). Soon after this, Schumann heard him play them and said that his playing of *The Fountain* created an effect 'almost magical'.

I ought to tell you how it was that he was able to accept Mendelssohn's invitation to go to Germany. The great piano firm of Broadwood (which, of course, still exists) came forward and said that if he would like to go they would pay the expense of the visit. That was generous and very wise expenditure; it is always a good thing for a young musician to travel and hear music in other countries and meet musicians of other nationalities.

Bennett went several times to Germany and enjoyed his association there with Mendelssohn and Schumann. Here is a funny Canon he wrote one night, after his Concert Overture *The Naiads* had been played at a great concert in Leipzig. Schumann and he and some friends had retired, after the concert, to an old inn, and there Bennett wrote this, and perhaps the others sang it (I have translated the words into English for you. The original is to be found in Sterndale Bennett's Life, by his son, published in 1907 by the Cambridge University Press):

A Description of Schumann

How they sang the treble part of this I do not know—unless there were some boys or ladies present. *You* can sing it, in a pretty effective sort of way, with *all* treble voices, if you like, but if you do so I should advise you to tell those who sing the upper stave to end on B (as shown in brackets), instead of on A.

Bennett's Later Years

Right through all three parts of this book I am telling you more about the youth of the musicians than about their later life, because I think that will interest you most, and now, having told you about Bennett's youth at some length, I must pass more quickly over his later years.

Bennett had to teach, and to do it all day and every day. This is the sort of life he led in his middle years. He gave his first lesson at seven or eight o'clock in the morning, and with short breaks for meals went on giving lessons until ten or eleven o'clock at night. A few of his lessons he gave at home, but most of them he gave at schools or at the houses of pupils, and he had a horse carriage with books and music to study as he went along, and often food for his meals. One day every week he was awakened at four o'clock by the policeman, so that he could catch the early train to Brighton, and there he worked hard all day, teaching piano in a school, not getting home again until eleven o'clock at night. Yet he kept cheerful with all this hard work, and really loved his teaching, taking the greatest pains with all his many pupils. The pupils said that he took as much interest in every piece he taught them as though it were a new piece he had never seen before. But of course this 'grind' checked his composition, and at last quite stopped it.

What Bennett Did for Bach

Although he was so busy, Bennett found time to do an excellent piece of work in showing the London musicians the beauties of Bach's music, which was still very little known in Britain. He founded a Bach Society, and gave the first performance in this country of the great *St. Matthew Passion.*

Honours Come

Of course, people realized what a good musician and fine man Bennett was, and honours of one sort and another came to him.

He was appointed Professor of Music at Cambridge University, and did a very good work there (he did not need to live at Cambridge, but only to visit it occasionally).

For ten years he was conductor of the Philharmonic Society in London—a very important appointment.

And he was made Principal of his old school, the Royal Academy of Music.

And at last Queen Victoria gave him a knighthood, and he became Sir William Sterndale Bennett.

But he did not earn very much money. For his Cambridge Professorship there was, for a long time, no stipend, and from the Royal Academy he would not take much, as it was short of funds, so for years he received for all his hard and valuable work there only about £20 a year! Bennett was a very self-denying man, and did not mind how hard he worked, or how little he received for his work, if he felt that what he was doing was for the good of music.

His Death

Bennett died comparatively young—at the age of fifty-nine. He was buried in Westminster Abbey, and there you can see his tombstone in the North Choir Aisle. Whilst you are in the Abbey, look, too, for the memorial of Purcell. Sullivan and Arne, two other British musicians who have chapters to themselves in this book, are buried respectively in St. Paul's Cathedral and St. Paul's Church, Covent Garden.

Bennett's Compositions

Besides a fair amount of piano music, Bennett wrote several Concert Overtures (*The Naiads, The Wood Nymphs, Paradise and the Peri*), a Symphony, some Piano Concertos and Orchestral works, a sacred Cantata (*The Woman of Samaria*), and a few songs. Hear any of this music that you can, and remember that in composing it Sterndale Bennett did us another great service in showing that an Englishman may be a fine musician.

The style of Bennett's music is, as you would expect, something like that of Mendelssohn. It is elegant and charming, not strong and forceful. But the composer's own individuality comes out in it, too. Schumann spoke of Bennett in his earlier days as 'a thorough Englishman, a glorious artist, and a beautiful and poetic soul.'

QUESTIONS

(To See Whether You Remember the Chapter and Understand It)

1. Why did Bennett never quite fulfil his early promise?

2. Where did his family come from?

3. Was it a musical family?

4. What was Bennett's first musical position?

5. How did he come to be a Londoner?

6. Tell anything you remember about life at the Royal Academy of Music in its early days.

7. Of whom was Bennett a 'grand-pupil'?

8. Who was the great German musician who 'discovered' Bennett?

9. How did Bennett manage to get to Germany?

10. Why was it important in those days that a young musician should go there?

11. And why is it now nothing like so important?

12. What effect had Bennett's recognition in Germany upon his recognition at home?

13. What great musician was still insufficiently appreciated here in Bennett's day?

14. And what did Bennett do to remedy this?

15. What honour came at last to Bennett?

16. Mention some of his compositions—all you can recall.

17. Is his music to be described as 'powerful'?

18. What (roughly) were Bennett's dates of birth and death?

THINGS TO DO

Find a pianist who knows some of Bennett's music and make him or her play it to you. Thus try to get an idea of what his style is like.

CHAPTER X

PARRY

1848-1918

No doubt some of the readers of this book have sung school songs by Parry, or, perhaps, played some of his piano pieces, and will be glad to know something about him.

Like Arne, more than a century earlier, Hubert Parry was an Eton boy. His father was a well-to-do man in Gloucestershire, a good amateur painter and the author of books on art and other subjects.

Hubert had begun to compose chants and hymn-tunes when he was eight, and a little later he had heard the great organist Samuel Sebastian Wesley play, which had increased his already great enthusiasm for music.

A School-Boy Musician

Whilst at Eton he spent a good deal of time at music, and when his voice broke it soon settled again, into a good baritone. He became quite famous amongst his school-fellows for his singing and playing and composing. When he was nineteen, and whilst still at school, he took his Bachelor of Music degree at Oxford University. He then left Eton for Oxford, and took his B.A. degree after the usual three years of study, and then went to London, where he went into business in the City. But he felt he must be a musician, not a business man, so after three years he left office work and began to spend his time in music.

The Beginnings of a Reputation

When he was about thirty-two Parry's name began to be known to people as that of a talented composer. A Piano Concerto of his was played at the famous Crystal Palace Concerts, and various choral works were sung at the Gloucester Festival. The first of these choral works was one which is still sung, a setting of Milton's poem, 'At a Solemn Musick', called by Parry (from its opening words) *Blest Pair of Sirens*. This is for eight unaccompanied sets of voices, which are wonderfully combined, so that the effect is very thrilling. Hear it, if you can!

Later, Parry wrote a good many Oratorios, some Orchestral Music, some Chamber Music, a large number of Songs, and some Piano Pieces. In all these things there are interesting passages and much fine music, but few of them have become popular, and some are already falling out of use. They have dignity and sometimes humour, and are very well composed, but in some cases lack real life, perhaps because their composer did not give himself enough time for composition, but occupied himself in so many other ways. What were these ways?

Parry's Busy Life

Well, first of all, when he was thirty-five, Parry was appointed assistant to Sir John Stainer, the Professor of Music at Oxford University, and when he was fifty-two he succeeded Stainer and himself became Professor. Meantime, when he was forty-six, he had become Director of the Royal College of Music, a very important

SIR HUBERT PARRY

ON BOARD THE 'WANDERER'

position, and one that took much time, for he wished to do his duties very thoroughly. Then he took to writing books, good ones, which you should some day read, such as:

Studies of Great Composers. This is meant for young people.

The Evolution of the Art of Music. This is too difficult for you at present, but you should read it when you grow older.

The Seventeenth Century. A volume in the great Oxford History of Music.

Style in Music. A very fine book, too little read.

John Sebastian Bach. (Parry was a great Bach enthusiast.)

A Summary of Musical History. This is only a good 'cram' book, suitable for people who are going in for musical examinations, or who want to get hold of the dates of the history of music as a basis for their further reading.

Queen Victoria made Parry a Knight and King Edward VII made him a Baronet. Parry well deserved these national honours, and everybody was glad when he got them, for every one admired the splendid work he was doing, especially as head of the Royal College of Music.

Parry and His Students

Parry's influence on the College students was very great. He was always very sympathetic with all of them, and by his support and example encouraged them to work hard and to aim at the highest possible.

He hated any sort of shams, and liked people to be thoroughly genuine.

Bad music he detested, for he felt it really did harm to people's characters to listen to what was cheap and base.

He was interested in the whole of life and not merely in music, and tried to make his students widen their lives in all possible ways. He had no patience with a musician who was *only* a musician; he wanted musicians to be broad-minded, well-educated, thinking men and women.

He believed in plenty of sport and was a good athlete as a young man, and a great yachtsman and swimmer in later life.

Parry was one of the most good-humoured, cheerful, friendly men one could ever meet, and to shake his hand and have a word or two of conversation with him always cheered one up and made one feel 'ready for anything.'

Some of Parry's Sayings

Here are a few paragraphs taken from the Addresses he used to give to the Royal College students at the opening of each term's work.

I

'The happiest people are those who have the widest outlook.'

II

'There is nothing better for musicians than to cultivate literary tastes, poetry, history, even philosophy.'

III

'An enormous waste of life comes about from our not taking our opportunities to see into things that come in our way. People take to spending their lives in such unprofitable futilities as card-playing, and even worse, because they have not had energy enough to look sensibly at the things that happen round them every day.'

IV

'A specialist is liable to see all life out of one window and not to know what it looks like out of another window. He may know his own subject all right, but when he comes across a man who is equally engrossed in another special subject, the two are mutually unintelligible.'

V

But though Parry wanted musicians to take an interest in other subjects than music, he did not approve of their dabbling first in one subject and then in another:

'Mere dissipation of energy is completely futile. It is deplorable when a man has so little power of coherence and concentration that at one moment he is studying geology, the next painting in water-colours, and the next listening eagerly to the theories of a fad doctor, and the next practising a mouth-organ, and the next studying the pedigrees of race-horses.'

VI

Can you see what Parry meant when he said:

'It is better to be a rebel than a slave'?

VII

'On the whole there is something even more chivalrous and fine about loyalty to an enemy and a rival than to people who merely engage our personal interest and regard. Such loyalty means readiness to admit and welcome whatever is well and honestly done, wherever we come across it, especially in rivals and adversaries if we have any.'

VIII

'The beauty of order is that there is so much more room for things. If you have twenty letters by post of a morning, and open them and throw them all down helter-skelter on the table, they look perfectly awful—it looks as if it would be best to put them in the waste-paper basket at once, and not try to answer them. But if you put them in a few piles, in accordance with the nature of their contents, they look ever so much smaller, and you don't despair of answering them all. Now one of your first objects in life is to get as much into it as you can. When you get old enough to look back, you will get a bit worried not to have done some things that were worth doing, and it is always well to remember we each have a little spell to get things done, and we do not get the chance to get them done again. The older you get, the shorter you will find your one chance; and the only way to pack life as full as it will hold is to put its contents into some sort of order. But there is no order that does for every one, and every one has to find the order that suits his disposition best—and that is where the room comes for your impulses and queernesses.'

IX

'Most of us are capable of being idiots at times. You will remember the familiar saying that "people who do not make mistakes do not make anything." You cannot have personal initiative without risk of making mistakes; and you cannot get things done without personal initiative.'

X

'If people make mistakes, that is useful too. For those who have any sense at all can learn as much from making mistakes as from anything else they make or mar.'

XI

'The man who is too greedy for appreciation too often produces not the best he might do if he were perfectly sincere, but the thing which will get him credit with a lot of people who are incapable of really judging whether what he does is good or bad. The poor thing thirsts for sympathy, and would sacrifice everything—his happiness and cleanliness of mind and his general well-being and his good relations with really intelligent friends, and all that really makes life worth living—to get it. And the result is that the appreciation he gets is less worth having every day he lives. For as he goes on adapting his achievements to those who have no understanding, he goes on making them stupider day by day, and his own work becomes worse and worse as it follows their increasing dullness; and he ends by being little better than a crazy egotist, who has lost the capacity to do things well and lives only to heal his excitable dupes pouring hysterical flatteries into his ears. The craving stupidly gratified becomes a kind of disease, and the pretence of great achievement a mockery.'

XII

'A man establishes his definite identity by making consistent and sensible use of such qualities and aptitudes and impulses as he has. He cannot alter them or pick and choose what he will have, any more than he can pick and choose his parents. But he can direct them.'

QUESTIONS

(To See Whether You Remember the Chapter and Understand It)

1. When was Parry born?

2. When did he die?

3. Mention any facts about his school life.

4. What did he do when he left school?

5. Give the name of a great choral work of his.

6. What important educational positions did he hold?

7. So far as you can make out from what I have told you, what sort of a fellow *was* Parry?

8. Was he the sort you would have liked to know?

THINGS TO DO

1. Get Parry's set of British Tunes arranged for Piano Duet and practise them with a friend. They are pretty easy. (Published by Augener.)

2. Or, if you are a fairly good player, get his *Shulebrede Tunes* and practise those. (Same publishers.)

3. Ask the conductor of your local Choral Society when he is going to perform *Blest Pair of Sirens*, and promise to buy a ticket when he does so if he'll let you come to one or two rehearsals as well as the proper performance—so that you can get to know the music well.

4. Get your English teacher to set as a subject for an essay one of the Parry sayings quoted in this chapter.

A LITTLE DICTIONARY OF BRITISH COMPOSERS OF OUR OWN TIMES

As I did not want to make the three parts of this book too big for you to read, the only chapters on British Composers of our own day and recent times that I have included in them are those on Sullivan (Second Book), Parry (Third Book), and Elgar (First Book). But therc are many others about whom you will from time to time wish to know something, especially if you chance to hear one of their works, or, perhaps, to have one given you to learn for your Piano lesson, or to practise in your school Singing Class or Choral Society.

The list I have made below is not for reading, but for reference. Of course you can read it through if you like, and if you do, so much the better, but the idea is that this is a sort of short Biographical Dictionary to which you can turn whenever you want to know whether a modern British Composer in whose music you are interested is living or dead, or old or young, and when you want to know something about his life and what music he has written.

RALPH VAUGHAN WILLIAMS

But we have hundreds of composers, and to pick amongst them those I should include in my list has been difficult. However, in the end I think I have been able to decide on a choice that includes all the best British Composers of our own day whose work you are likely to come across. But of course a list like this will be always getting out of date, and so in every edition of this book that comes out (if other editions are called for) there will have to be changes and additions.

AUSTIN, Ernest. Born in London in 1874. On leaving school he became a business man, and only took up composition as a profession when he was over thirty. He is almost self-taught in music. His compositions include some Orchestral pieces and Choral music, a good deal of Chamber Music, a big 'narrative-poem' in twelve parts, for the Organ, called *The Pilgrim's Progress*, Songs and a great deal of Piano music, much of it especially composed for children's playing. (Frederic Austin, the singer and composer, is his brother.)

BAINTON, Edgar L. Born in 1880, and trained at the Royal College of Music. Bainton is Principal of the Conservatoire of Music at Newcastle-on-Tyne, and conductor of the Philharmonic Orchestra in that city. He has written many Orchestral works, Piano pieces, Choral works, Songs and Part Songs (many of these especially for school use), etc. During the war he was one of the little band of English musicians who were interned at Ruhleben, and who busied themselves in all kinds of musical activities there.

BANTOCK, Granville. Born in London, 1868. His father was a well-known surgeon. Granville was trained as a chemical engineer, but neglected his engineering work and gave much of his time to music. The Principal of the College where he was studying pointed this out to the father and persuaded him that the boy was meant by nature to be a musician. He was then sent to the Royal Academy of Music, where he did *not* neglect music for chemical engineering, but worked hard at his proper studies for four years, composing a great deal of music whilst still a student there.

On leaving the Academy Bantock started a musical paper, called the *New Quarterly Musical Review*, which lived for three years. Meanwhile he did a good deal of work as conductor of touring theatrical companies, including one engagement that took him round the world. In San Francisco he went one night to see the Chinese quarters, and was chased by rowdies who shot at him with revolvers, but he escaped them. When he came home he brought with him an ape, a parrot, and other animals and birds. Soon after his return he married a poetess, and he has set to music many of her poems. Then he became conductor of the band at the Tower, New Brighton, near Liverpool.

All this time he was composing all sorts of music. He conducted a Choral Society at this time, and so got experience which helped him in writing very fine pieces of Choral music in later life. When he was thirty-two Bantock was appointed Principal of the great School of Music at Birmingham, and this position he still holds. He is also Professor of Music at Birmingham University.

GRANVILLE BANTOCK

Bantock has written

1. A great many Songs.
2. A great many Part Songs.
3. Some Two-Part Songs and Unison Songs, for children.
4. A good many arrangements for Chorus of old Folk-Songs.
5. Choral Music on a big scale, such as *Omar Khayyam* (Chorus and Orchestra), and *Vanity of Vanities* (for Chorus alone), and *Atalanta in Calydon* (Chorus alone).
6. Orchestral Music, such as *Fifine at the Fair, The Pierrot of the Minute, Old English Suite*, and the great *Hebridean Symphony*, the chief musical 'subjects' of which are Hebridean Folk-tunes.

A good many of Bantock's songs and other pieces are Oriental or Scottish in their subjects.

Bantock has also edited a good deal of Elizabethan choral and instrumental music. Readers who can play the piano decently should get the keyboard works of (1) Bull, (2) Byrd, (3) Farnaby, as edited by him and published by Novello (especially get Farnaby).

BAX, Arnold, was born in London in 1883. He studied at the Royal College of Music. He has written:

1. Much Orchestral Music, such as *The Garden of Fand* and *November Woods.*
2. Some good *Chamber Music.*

3. A number of Piano Pieces, including two Sonatas and many short and attractive things.

4. A very large number of SONGS.

BLISS, Arthur. Born in London in 1891. Educated at Rugby and Cambridge. A very original sort of composer who goes his own way and composes in new styles to please himself. His music includes a *Piano Quintet*, music for theatre performances of Shakespeare's *The Tempest*, some Songs, a *Rhapsody* for Tenor and Mezzo-Soprano voices, with Flute, Oboe, and String Quartet, *Rout*, a rowdy, jolly piece for Mezzo-Soprano voice, Flute, Clarinet, String Quartet, Double Bass, Harp, Side Drum, and Glockenspiel. A *Concerto* for Tenor voice, Piano, Strings, and Percussion. *Conversations* for Violin, Viola, 'Cello, Flute, Bass Flute, Oboe, Cor Anglais, and Piano (not all used at one time; one of the pieces is an unaccompanied solo for Cor Anglais: the names of the different 'Conversations' are 'The Committee', 'In the Wood', 'At the Ball', 'Soliloquy', and 'In the Tube at Oxford Circus'); *A Colour Symphony*.

You will notice in that list the unusual combinations of instruments sometimes used. This is characteristic of the composer, and so is the use of the voice *as an instrument amongst other instruments*, and without words.

BOUGHTON, Rutland. Born in 1878. He studied music at the Royal College of Music, and then went to teach singing in the Birmingham School of Music of which Bantock is Principal.

A friend of Boughton's, named Reginald Buckley, wrote the poems for a great 'cycle' of Music Dramas, on the subject of King Arthur, and Boughton started to set these to music. He then went and settled in Glastonbury (where King Arthur is supposed to have lived), and every year held musical festivals, at which he gradually brought out some of these music dramas. He hoped to build a special theatre there for the purpose, but the war spoilt all the plans and he has not yet succeeded.

Now he lives at Bristol, where he carries on his Festival School, but Festivals are still held at Glastonbury in summer time. One of his ideas is that the young people of Glastonbury shall take as much part as possible in the singing and acting and dancing of these dramas about the legends of their own district, and in the other music dramas and performances of various kinds which he gives there.

Boughton's works include:

1. STAGE WORKS—*The Immortal Hour* (this has proved very popular and has been a great deal performed in various parts of the country), *The Birth of Arthur, The Round Table, Bethlehem* (a Christmas 'Nativity Play'), *Alcestis.*

2. SONGS.

3. A little CHAMBER MUSIC, PIANO MUSIC, etc.

4. Some PART SONGS (Boughton was the first to think of the good idea of arranging British Folk-songs with Choral Variations).

BOWEN, York. Born in London, 1884. Studied for seven years at the Royal Academy of Music. His works include Orchestral Music, Chamber Music, Songs, and a large number of Piano pieces.

BRIDGE, Frank. Born at Brighton in 1879. Studied at the Royal College of Music. He is a very fine Viola player and takes part in a great deal of Chamber Music playing.

His music includes:

ORCHESTRAL WORKS. A Suite, *The Sea*, and a *Lament* for String Orchestra (to commemorate a little girl who was drowned in the *Lusitania*) with many other pieces.

CHAMBER MUSIC. A great many Quartets, etc. The pieces that would be most enjoyed by younger listeners are *An Irish Melody* (an arrangement for String Quartet of the famous and beautiful 'Londonderry Air') and three books of *Miniatures*, for Piano and Violin and 'Cello (easy to play; published by Goodwin & Tabb).

PIANO PIECES. A great many short pieces (published by Augener and Rogers).

VIOLIN PIECES. A number (published by Augener and Rogers).

SONGS. A good many, including a number of School songs (published by Rogers).

CARSE, Adam. Born at Newcastle-on-Tyne in 1878, and trained at the Royal Academy of Music. He has written two Symphonies and many other Orchestral works, several Cantatas, many Songs, a good deal of Piano Music and Violin Music (some of it especially for young people), and books of studies for the Violin and other things. The name on some of his music appears as A. von Ahn Carse. I mention the fact lest you should think this to be another composer.

COLERIDGE-TAYLOR, Samuel. Born in London, 1875; died 1912. Coleridge-Taylor's father was a West African negro, who came to England, was trained as a doctor of medicine, and practised here. He married an English girl. When Samuel was a few years old, his father, who had been unsuccessful as a doctor in England, went back to West Africa, and the mother and child had no money to live on.

But the people with whom they lodged (at Croydon, near London) were very kind to them, and so they managed to live, in a very simple way indeed, they and the kind man and woman who supported them having only three rooms amongst them.

When Samuel was five years old the man gave him a small-sized violin, and this was a great delight to him. He had a few cheap lessons in violin playing, and learnt to play easy things. One day the conductor of the Croydon Orchestra, looking out of the window, saw a curly-haired black boy playing marbles in the street, and holding in one hand a little fiddle. He went out and persuaded him to come in and play some simple violin duets with him, and was so pleased with his playing that he said he would give him music lessons for nothing, and for seven years he did so. When Coleridge-Taylor could play well enough his teacher made him play at a concert; there were ferns and plants along the front of the platform, and the boy was so small that they had

SAMUEL COLERIDGE-TAYLOR

to put a box for him to stand on or the audience would not have been able to see him.

At school Coleridge-Taylor's nickname was 'Coaley'. His teacher was very keen on singing, and taught the boys to read well at sight. He used to make 'Coaley' stand on a table and play an accompaniment to the school songs.

At the Presbyterian Church in Croydon at that time a Colonel Walters was the choirmaster, and his brother was the organist. Colonel Walters used to look out for the boys who could sing and the headmaster of the school told him of 'Coaley', who was then admitted to the choir and soon became solo boy. Colonel Walters was very good to him, and used to ask him to come to his house to learn more about music.

Colonel Walters had faith in him and believed he would some day be a great musician, and so when his schooldays were over he sent him to study at the Royal College of Music. Here he studied Violin, Piano, and Composition. His chief teacher of Composition was Stanford. By and by he gained a scholarship at the College. He was still very poor, and one of the things that the writer of his biography remembers is 'a large circular patch on his trousers.'

When Coleridge-Taylor was about twenty, the negro American poet, Paul Lawrence Dunbar (of whom you may read something when you are older) came to England, and Coleridge-Taylor and he gave some recitals together, Dunbar reciting his poems and Coleridge-Taylor having some of his compositions performed. Coleridge-Taylor was proud of being a negro, and the negroes in America (a very musical race) were proud of him. He went to America in later years to perform some of his music, and I have been told by people there that the negroes followed him about so closely that the white people could hardly get near him.

The first real recognition that Coleridge-Taylor got as a composer came through Elgar, who had been asked to compose a short orchestral piece for the Gloucester Festival. He wrote and told the Committee that he was too busy to do this and begged them to let Coleridge-Taylor do it instead, because, he said, 'he is by far the cleverest fellow amongst the young men.' The work Coleridge-Taylor wrote for Gloucester is the *Ballad in A Minor*. It was very much praised in all the papers and brought his name into notice for the first time.

Soon after this Coleridge-Taylor's choral-orchestral work *Hiawatha's Wedding-Feast* (a setting of parts of Longfellow's well-known poem) was performed at a College Concert. This was a very great success. Sullivan, then a dying man, was present, and praised the work highly. From this moment Coleridge-Taylor was famous, and here I may leave my account of his life, of which you may read a fuller account, if you wish, in the book *Samuel Coleridge-Taylor*, by W. C. Berwick Sayers (Cassell), which is out of print but can be seen in libraries.

Coleridge-Taylor died very young—at thirty-seven. He left a widow and two children, and the negro musical people of America, who were so proud of him, with help from a few other people, bought the house in which

Coleridge-Taylor had been living and gave it to them.

Coleridge-Taylor's chief works are:

CANTATAS. *Hiawatha's Wedding-Feast; The Death of Minnehaha; Hiawatha's Departure* (all these three are settings of parts of Longfellow's poem); *A Tale of Old Japan.*

ORCHESTRAL WORKS. A Symphony, a Violin Concerto, *Four Characteristic Waltzes*, and many other things.

CHAMBER MUSIC.

VIOLIN MUSIC.

SONGS.

PART SONGS.

ORGAN MUSIC.

PIANO PIECES (these include *Twenty-Four Negro Melodies, transcribed for Piano Solo*).

DALE, Benjamin. Born in London, 1885. He studied at the Royal Academy of Music, and is now a Professor of that institution. During the war he was interned by the Germans at Ruhleben. He has not published a great deal of music. Some of his pieces are for the Viola, an instrument usually neglected by composers; these include an *Introduction and Andante for Six Violas*—surely the only piece ever written for such a combination. His *Piano Sonata in D Minor* is a long and fine work which attracted a great deal of attention in 1905 when it appeared. (Readers for whom this is too difficult, and who possess a Piano-player, can make acquaintance with it as a piano-player roll.)

DAVIES, (Sir) H. Walford. Born at Oswestry in 1869. When he was twelve, Sir H. Walford Davies became a choir-boy at St. George's Chapel in Windsor Castle, and when his voice broke he became assistant to the organist, Sir Walter Parratt. Then he won a scholarship at the Royal College of Music, and at the same time that he was carrying on his studies there he held various positions as organist in London churches.

When Sir Henry was twenty-nine he obtained a very important position—that of organist of the Temple Church. This is the old church of the Knights Templar, between the Strand and the Embankment, a famous old building that is now the church of the lawyers, who since the order of the Knights Templar was destroyed in the early fourteenth century have occupied their London headquarters. The music at the Temple Church is by many people thought to be the best Church music in England—and, therefore, probably in the world. For one thing the boys are beautifully trained, and when the Psalms are sung you can follow every word, even if you have no book. There are many special musical services in the Temple Church, and when they are held the church is always crowded.

Besides holding this post Sir H. Walford Davies also holds that of Professor of Music in the University of Wales. He is a rather unusual sort of professor, for he does not merely give lectures to students in the University and hold examinations, but visits all parts of Wales in his car, trying to make the country more musical by showing schoolmasters how to do better music teaching, by getting up concerts and so forth.

During the war Sir H. Walford Davies was a major in the Air Force, and his duties were to teach airmen how to keep themselves happy with singing and other music.

Sir H. Walford Davies's works include the Cantata *Everyman* and other fine choral pieces, a *Peter Pan* String Quartet, a good many *Nursery Rhymes* skilfully and humorously arranged for Vocal Quartet, a Children's Cantata, *Humpty Dumpy*, *A Solemn Melody* for Organ and Orchestra (you can get this as a Gramophone record), a number of Songs (some of them very popular, such as *The Jocund Dance* and *When Childher Play*). And he has edited a good book of songs for us all to sing when we gather together—*The Fellowship Song Book* (Curwen).

DELIUS, Frederick. Born at Bradford in 1863. His parents were German. When he was nineteen or twenty he went to Florida and became an orange-planter. As a keen musician, however, he spent all his spare time in studying music. After some time he left America and went to Germany to study at the great Leipzig School of Music (or 'Conservatory'). After this he lived mostly in France and spent his time in composing pieces which gradually made his name well known. Once he wrote some music for a Norwegian play, and when the play was performed in Christiania a man in the audience, who did not like the way he had brought the Norwegian National Anthem into his music, fired several revolver shots at him, but, fortunately, missed him.

Some of Delius's chief works are these:

Operas. *Koanga, A Village Romeo and Juliet, Fennimore and Gerda.*

Orchestral Pieces. *Paris, Brigg Fair, On Hearing the First Cuckoo in Spring* (this is a very favourite piece), *Summer Night on the River,* a *Piano Concerto,* a *Violin Concerto,* a *Double Concerto for Violin and 'Cello, Appalachia* (this ends with a chorus).

Choral Pieces. *Sea Drift, A Mass of Life, a Requiem,* and *The Song of the High Hills.*

There are also some pieces of Chamber Music and some Songs.

DUNHILL, Thomas. Born in London, 1877. He was trained at the Royal College of Music, and then became an assistant music-master at Eton. He is now a Professor at the Royal College of Music. Some years ago he gave a great many concerts in order to make known the works of the younger British composers.

Dunhill's works include some Orchestral Music and a good deal of Chamber Music, some Piano pieces (including a good many easy ones, specially written for children), a large number of Songs (including songs for school singing classes), and a very useful book about Chamber Music.

FARJEON, Harry. Born (of British parents) in New Jersey (U.S.A.) in 1878. His father was a well-known novelist. Farjeon was trained at the Royal Academy of Music. He has composed a great deal of music of all kinds, including Singing Games for Children (Augener), much Piano music (some of it for children), Songs, Orchestral pieces, etc.

GARDINER, H. Balfour. Born in London, 1877. He was educated at Charterhouse School and Oxford, and then went to Germany to study music. Afterwards he became a music master at Winchester College, but has now retired from work of this sort and lives quietly in the country. Being a well-to-do and generous man he has frequently held concerts specially in order that the younger British composers should have a chance of performing their Orchestral works.

Balfour Gardiner has written a good deal of attractive Orchestral Music (you can get his jolly *Shepherd Fennel's Dance* as a Gramophone record), some Songs and a good many Part Songs, and very popular and good Piano pieces, such as the *Preludes* and a *Noël* (with a Christmas tune in it).

GERMAN, Edward. Born at Whitchurch in Shropshire in 1862. When he was a youth he got up a village band, which used to perform at concerts in the countryside around where he lived. He also taught himself to play the Violin. Then he went to study at the Royal Academy of Music, and after this he played the Violin in Orchestras in theatres and concert-halls for a time. Then he was made musical director of a London theatre, and began composing music for some of the plays. The music he wrote for Shakespeare's 'Henry VIII' made him very popular (you can get some of it for Piano or for Gramophone). His light opera *Merrie England* was a great success; he has also written a good many other light operas, as well as Symphonies and Suites and a *Welsh Rhapsody*, Songs and Part Songs.

Nearly all his music is light and pleasing rather than serious and solemn.

GOOSSENS, Eugene. Born in London in 1893. His grandfather was a Belgian and also called Eugene; he was a well-known opera conductor. His father is also called Eugene, and is also a well-known opera conductor. Eugene III studied at the Bruges Conservatory of Music, at the Liverpool College of Music, and at the Royal College of Music. He became a very good violinist and played for some years in the Queen's Hall Orchestra. Then he took up conducting and became assistant conductor to Sir Thomas Beecham. In 1921 he founded an Orchestra of his own, which is sometimes heard in London. He is also one of the conductors of the National Opera Company. Goossens's works include some very good Chamber Music, some Songs and Piano pieces, and some Orchestral pieces. His later music is very modern in style.

GRAINGER, Percy Aldridge. Born in Melbourne in Australia in 1882. His mother was his first teacher, but he afterwards travelled in Germany and had lessons from some famous pianists there. When he was eighteen he came to England and played at many concerts. In Norway he became a very great friend of Grieg, who, when he was dying, asked the Committee of the Leeds Festival to let Grainger play the Grieg Concerto, as he was himself too ill to be able to keep his promise to do so: Grieg died a few weeks before the Festival took place. Grieg's interest in Norwegian Folk-tunes made Grainger interested in British Folk-tunes, and he has written some very jolly pieces made out of such tunes. For instance there is a String Quartet called *Molly on the Shore*, which is made out of Irish Reels, and a piece (to be had either for Orchestra or Piano) called *Shepherd's Hey*, made out of English Folk-dance tunes, and there are some Part Songs which are 'arrangements' of Folk-songs. During the war Grainger became a citizen of the United States.

HOLBROOKE, Joseph. Born in London in 1878. He was trained at the Royal Academy of Music. He has written some Music Dramas, a good many works for Chorus and Orchestra, a great deal of Orchestral Music (you can get his *Three Blind Mice* as a very effective Gramophone record), a lot of Chamber Music, and many Songs, Part Songs, and Piano pieces. The list of his compositions is, indeed, enormous.

HOLST, Gustav. Born in Cheltenham in 1874. (His original name was 'von Holst', but he dropped the 'von' when he went out during the war to do musical work amongst the soldiers in Salonica and Constantinople. He is not German by descent, as people have thought, but one of his four great-grandfathers, a long time ago, came to England from the Baltic provinces of Russia.)

Holst's father was a Pianist and Organist. He sent his son to the Royal College of Music, where he became a pupil of Stanford. On leaving the College, Holst joined the Carl Rosa Opera Company as a trombonist and also as a sort of sub-conductor; then he joined the Scottish

GUSTAV HOLST

Orchestra, and afterwards he became Musical Director at Morley College (a College for working men and women, just a little south of the Thames at Waterloo Bridge). Here he does splendid work conducting a Choir and Orchestra and teaching the students to compose. All his pupils there like him very much because he throws himself heartily into the work and makes them work heartily too. He has made Morley College a notable centre for the study and performance of the works of Byrd and Purcell. He is also Music Master at the great St. Paul's School for Girls, at Hammersmith, and a Professor of Composition at the Royal College of Music.

Holst's works include:

OPERAS, such as *Savitri* and *The Perfect Fool.*

ORCHESTRAL PIECES, especially *The Planets*, which has been performed in many parts of the world.

CHORAL MUSIC, such as the *Hymn of Jesus* and *Ode to Death.*

MILITARY BAND MUSIC. Most people neglect the military band, but Holst does not, and this is a good thing, for far more people hear Military Band Music than hear Orchestral Music, and the music written for such bands ought, therefore, always to be good.

SONGS AND PART SONGS—quite a lot (some of the later solo songs have accompaniment for a Violin only, which is a new idea).

HOWELLS, Herbert. Born at Lydney in Gloucestershire, 1892. Studied at the Royal College of Music, of which he is now a Professor. His works include a Piano Concerto, a piece for Orchestra and Chorus, *Sine Nomine*, Orchestral pieces, *Lady Audrey's Suite* for String Quartet, and other Chamber Music, and some Piano and Organ pieces.

IRELAND, John. Born at Bowdon, Cheshire, in 1879. His father was editor of the *Manchester Examiner*. He was trained at the Royal College of Music. His works include a fine (and very difficult) Piano Sonata and many smaller pieces, such as *The Island Spell* (one of a set of pieces called 'Decorations'), *Chelsea Reach, Ragamuffin,* and *Soho Forenoons,* a good deal of Chamber Music, Orchestral pieces, *The Forgotten Rite,* and *Rhapsody*, and a good many Songs, including some for school use (Year Book Press, Curwen, Stainer & Bell).

MACKENZIE, (Sir) Alexander Campbell. Born at Edinburgh in 1847, into a very musical family; his great-grandfather played in a Militia Band, his grandfather was a Violinist, and so was his father, who was leader of the Orchestra in an Edinburgh theatre.

When the future Sir Alexander was only ten he was sent to Germany to study music. Here he learnt to play the Violin and to compose, and played in an orchestra. When he came back, at the age of fifteen, he had forgotten his native language and had to learn it again. He then won a scholarship at the Royal Academy of Music, where he stayed until he was eighteen. Meantime he earned some money and got further experience by playing in various theatre orchestras in London. When he left the Academy he was quickly recognized as a fine Solo Violinist. He settled for a time in Scotland and

SIR ALEXANDER MACKENZIE

conducted a Choral Society, acted as Precentor in an Edinburgh church, gave concerts, and composed.

By and by Mackenzie felt he was working too hard at these activities and not composing enough, so he went and settled in Italy (at Florence). There he stayed ten years, though of course he often visited London and performed there, or superintended the performance there of his compositions. When he was forty-one he was appointed Principal of the Royal Academy of Music, his own old school, and there, at the time this book is written, he still remains.

His works include:

OPERAS. *The Cricket on the Hearth*, and five or six more.

ORATORIOS AND CANTATAS. *The Rose of Sharon* and a dozen more.

ORCHESTRAL PIECES. *Britannia Overture* (you can get this as a Gramophone record), *London Day by Day* Suite, a *Violin Concerto*, a *Piano Concerto* and a very large number of other pieces.

SONGS AND PART SONGS. A great many (including some school songs).

PIANO PIECES AND VIOLIN PIECES. A fair number.

McEWEN, John B. Born at Harwich in Roxburghshire in 1868. He is a Professor at the Royal Academy of Music. His works include Symphonies, three or four Overtures (including *Grey Galloway*) and some Suites and Scottish Dances, a Concerto for Violin and another for Piano, a number of Cantatas, Chamber Music (a little of which you can get in the form of Gramophone records), Songs and Piano Music, and some theoretical books.

O'NEILL, Norman. Born in London, 1875. He has written many Orchestral pieces (and, especially, 'incidental music' for plays), Songs, Piano pieces, etc.

QUILTER, Roger. Born at Brighton, 1877. Educated at Eton, and musically trained in Germany. His Orchestral compositions include a very jolly *Children's Overture*, on nursery rhyme tunes (this can be got as Piano solo or duet, published by Rogers, or as a Gramophone record). He has also written very many Songs, and some Piano music and Violin music.

ROOTHAM, Cyril Bradley. Born in 1875 at Bristol, where his father was a very well-known musician. Educated at Clifton and at Cambridge, and trained in music at the Royal College of Music. He is a Doctor of Music, and is organist of St. John's College, Cambridge, and conductor of the University Musical Society. His music includes an Opera, *The Two Sisters*, many Orchestral and Choral pieces, Chamber Music, Songs, Part Songs, etc.

ROWLEY, Alec. Born in London in 1892. He has composed a great deal of Piano Music (much of it especially for children), and Organ Music, and some Songs (some for school use), and has edited some Old English Harpsichord Music, so that it may be played by Piano pupils.

SCOTT, Cyril. Born at Oxton in Cheshire in 1879. He was educated in Germany. His compositions include much Orchestral and Chamber Music, a very large number of Songs and much Piano Music, some of it suitable for moderately advanced piano pupils (Elkin). He has also published a volume of Poems and a book called *The Philosophy of Modernism in its Connection with Music.*

SHAW, Geoffrey Turton. Born in London, 1879. He was a choir-boy of St. Paul's Cathedral. He has composed a good deal of Church Music, and many School Songs, and is co-editor, with his brother Martin (see below), of several volumes of the *Motherland Song Book.* He is Inspector of Music to the Board of Education.

SHAW, Martin. Born in London, 1876. He studied at the Royal College of Music, and then held various positions as Organist and also as a theatrical conductor. He is now in charge of the music at St. Martin's Church, Trafalgar Square, and at the Guildhouse, Eccleston Square. He has composed various musical plays, such as *The Cockyolly Bird* and *Brer Rabbit and Mr. Fox*, and written the music for the children's Shakespeare plays, *The Pedlar* (from 'The Winter's Tale') and *The Fools and the Fairies* (from 'A Midsummer-Night's Dream'). He is the compiler and editor of *Songs of Britain.* His brother is Mr. Geoffrey Shaw, above mentioned.

SMYTH, (Dame) Ethel. Born at Sidcup, 1858; daughter of an artillery General. She studied music in Germany, and her earlier compositions were all performed there. She was a friend of Brahms. For some time her works were very little heard in her own country,

DAME ETHEL SMYTH

but now they are rather more frequently performed. She has written a number of Operas, which have been performed at various German Opera Houses and at the great Metropolitan Opera House in New York and at Covent Garden Opera House in London. Her comic opera *The Boatswain's Mate*, which is founded on a short story by W. W. Jacobs, has often been performed in England.

In 1910 Durham University made Miss Smyth a Doctor of Music, as a recognition of her work; in 1911 she was imprisoned for two months as a Women's Suffrage agitator; during the war she did radio work in France, and in 1920 the King, in recognition of her musical work, conferred on her the feminine equivalent of knighthood, so that she is now known as Dame Ethel Smyth. She has written a large and very interesting two-volume book about her life, called *Impressions that Remained*; and another shorter book, called *Streaks of Life*.

SOMERVELL, Arthur. Born at Windermere, 1863. He was educated at Uppingham and King's College, Cambridge, and trained in music in Berlin and at the Royal College of Music. Dr. Somervell has composed a large number of Orchestral and Choral works, Operettas, Songs, Part Songs, Piano pieces, etc., and also written many educational works. He is H.M. Chief Inspector of Music in Schools and Training Colleges, and has been the means of securing greater attention for British Folk-songs in British schools.

SIR CHARLES VILLIERS STANFORD

STANFORD, (Sir) Charles Villiers. Born at Dublin in 1852. His father was a good amateur singer and encouraged his musical bent.

At eight years old Charles composed a march, which a year or two later was performed in the pantomime, 'Puss in Boots,' at Dublin. When he was eighteen he went to Cambridge as a 'choral scholar' at Queen's College, that is to say, he had a scholarship given him in return for his services as a singer in the college choir. Later he was made organist of Trinity College, Cambridge, and from there he took his degree with Classical Honours. He became conductor of the Cambridge University Musical Society.

Then for a time he went to Germany to study, and when he came back he composed the music to one of Tennyson's plays, which was performed at the Lyceum Theatre in London. After this he composed a great many symphonies and choral works, which were given at the great Festivals and at Concerts in London. When he was thirty-five he was appointed Professor of Music at Cambridge University, and later he also became Professor of Composition at the Royal College of Music. King Edward knighted him in 1901.

Sir Charles Stanford's works include:

OPERAS. *Shamus O' Brien, The Critic, The Travelling Companion,* and six others.

CHORAL MUSIC. T*he Revenge, Phaudrig Crohoore, Requiem, The Last Post, Songs of the Sea, Songs of the Fleet,* and a great many other works.

ORCHESTRAL WORKS. Seven Symphonies, five Irish Rhapsodies, eight Concertos, and many other works.

CHAMBER MUSIC. Many Trios, Quartets, and Quintets.

SONGS AND PART SONGS, PIANO PIECES, VIOLIN PIECES, ORGAN PIECES, etc.

BOOKS. A very fine volume on Composition and two or three volumes of Reminiscences, etc.

As might be expected, much of Sir Charles Stanford's music has a flavour of Irish Folk-music; also, he has edited volumes of Irish Folk-songs.

SWINSTEAD, Felix. Born in London in 1889. Trained at the Royal Academy of Music. Swinstead has written a great many Piano pieces (some of them especially for young players) and also some Songs and Orchestral pieces.

WALKER, Ernest. Born at Bombay in 1870 and educated at Balliol College, Oxford, where since 1900 he has been Director of Music. Here he conducts a remarkable series of concerts on Sunday evenings in term time, to which members of the University may come, and he also helps to carry on the University Musical Club and Union, which holds weekly concerts. He is a Doctor of Music of Oxford University, has been 'Choragus' of the University, and is now University Lecturer in Harmony. He is also an Inspector in Music for the Girls' Public Day School Trust. His compositions include Songs, Choral Music, Chamber Music, etc.

WALLACE, William. Born at Greenock in 1860. His father was a surgeon and he became one too. Then he came to London, and studied for a short time at the Royal Academy of Music. During the war he served as an army doctor, and he still takes a great interest in hospital work. He has composed a number of fine Orchestral works, including a Symphonic Poem on William Wallace (his ancestor), and another, *Villon* (this can be obtained as a Pianola roll). He has also written many Songs, some of which, such as *Son of Mine* and the *Freebooters' Songs*, have become popular. He has also written two learned books on the working of the mind of the musician. They are called *The Threshold of Music and The Musical Faculty.*

WHITTAKER, William Gillies. Born at Newcastle-on-Tyne in 1876. At first he was a schoolmaster, and this taught him how to train children; then he was placed in charge of the music at Armstrong College, Newcastle, and there he had to train teachers. He also conducted several Choral Societies, and learnt to train amateur singers, and was Organist at various churches at various times. He now conducts the Bach Choir at Newcastle. He has composed a number of Songs, and arranged in a very effective way for choral singing many North Country Folk-songs, and he has compiled and edited a fine collection of Northumbrian Folk-songs, for use in schools and elsewhere. He has also published a very useful book for young pianists called *Time Studies* (Curwen). He is a Doctor of Music of Durham University.

WILLIAMS, Ralph Vaughan. Born at Down Ampney in Gloucestershire in 1872. He was educated at Cheltenham and Cambridge and trained in music at the Royal College of Music, and in Germany and France. He also pursued his musical studies amongst the village people of England, collecting their Folk-songs. This made him very fond of the 'Modes' (or old scales in which many of the Folk-songs are composed), and so his music is very often 'Modal', that is to say, it is often in one or other of these old scales. Dr. Vaughan Williams is a Professor of Composition at the Royal College of Music, and Conductor of the London Bach Choir. At the beginning of the war he enlisted as a private in the R.A.M.C. and served to the end of the war in various fields.

His works include:

OPERA. *Hugh the Drover* (Ballad Opera, i.e. an opera made out of old folk-tunes, interspersed with spoken dialogue).

ORCHESTRAL PIECES. *A London Symphony* (in this the composer gives us the spirit of London in various aspects); *Pastoral Symphony* (in this he gives us the spirit of the country as he feels it); Suite, *The Wasps; Fantasia on a Theme of Thomas Tallis* (for Strings alone), three *Norfolk Rhapsodies* and other works.

WORKS FOR CHORUS AND ORCHESTRA. *A Sea Symphony; Five Mystical Songs; Fantasia on Christmas Carols; Toward the Unknown Region.*

Songs. A good many, including some Song Cycles (that is songs meant to be performed as sets); one of these is *On Wenlock Edge*. (Dr. Vaughan Williams has also edited and published books of Folk-songs and Sea Songs. One book of Folk-songs is arranged specially for schools; it is published by Novello.)

Part Songs. A good many (and also some Folk-songs arranged for Men's Voices).

Chamber Music. A String Quartet and a String Quintet.

Organ Pieces. Three Preludes founded on Welsh Hymns and Melodies. Dr. Vaughan Williams has written an interesting pamphlet on *Folk-songs* (Joseph Williams), has edited some of Purcell's music, and has also edited *The English Hymnal*.

WILLIAMS, John Gerrard. Born at Catford in 1888. Gerrard Williams was trained as an architect, but preferred music. He has written two String Quartets and some other Chamber Music, a number of Songs and Part Songs, a little Orchestral Music, and some Piano Music. When he gave up Architecture he at once started composing very actively indeed, and became well known in an unusually short time.

www.ingramcontent.com/pod-product-compliance
Lightning Source LLC
LaVergne TN
LVHW090950080826
845145LV00003B/956

* 9 7 8 1 6 3 3 3 4 1 3 0 2 *